Leonard A. Robinson

LIGHT

at the tunnel end

by Leonard A. Robinson

Foundation for the Handicapped and Elderly, Inc.
1209 Burton Street
Silver Spring, Maryland 20910

1975

Standard Book Number 87012-198-7
Library of Congress Card Number 74-15985
Printed in the United States of America
Copyright © 1975 by Leonard A. Robinson
Silver Spring, Maryland
All Rights Reserved

Printed by
McClain Printing Company
Parsons, West Virginia

Dedication

It is with the greatest pleasure and pride that I dedicate this book to Senator Jennings Randolph of West Virginia. His native state can be as proud of him as are all the blind and other physically handicapped persons in the United States who have benefited greatly from his sponsorship of Federal legislation in Congress.

This outstanding member of Congress, who was then a member of the lower house, succeeded in doing what others of his congressional colleagues were unable to accomplish.

Today, Senator Randolph is the leading spokesman in Congress for all the physically handicapped, and the legislation which bears his name is bringing to countless thousands of handicapped persons security and peace of mind.

Contents

Senator Jennings Randolph

Foreword

Members of Congress frequently receive more credit than they deserve. If we are honest with ourselves, we must give credit to those who call needs to our attention—and help us to work out solutions to those needs.

Such a man is Leonard Robinson, whose dedicated labor over the past half century on behalf of the blind has resulted in a body of progressive law and a commendable change in public attitudes toward the visually handicapped.

This book is a culmination of his many years of effort to help his fellowman. He has given new vision to those of us who are sighted. He convinced me long ago of the need to assist the blind in achieving the dignity of work.

As chairman of the Senate Subcommittee on the Handicapped, I am particularly concerned with the problem of employment opportunities for the blind. This is a task to which I have devoted much effort. In 1935, as a member of the United States House of Representatives, I was privileged to coauthor with Senator Morris Sheppard of Texas the legislation which established the blind vending stand program.

I am gratified my name has been attached to this landmark legislation over the past thirty-nine years. It has been acknowledged as one of the most successful Federal laws which has provided—at minimum expense to the taxpayer—opportunities to many thousands of blind persons to become self-supporting, tax-paying citizens. They have demonstrated to the public that individuals with this extreme handicap can become capable and productive workers.

The story of the Randolph-Sheppard blind vendors program needs to be told, and no one person is more intimately involved, more knowledgeable of the program and its potential, than the author of this book.

In successfully proving to the Congress and to the public that the blind can, with training, become independent, productive citizens, the Randolph-Sheppard program served as a cutting edge for the creation of other legislation to aid the handicapped.

The heartening change in public attitudes over the past three decades was brought about principally by the achievements of the handicapped themselves. No product can survive in our marketplace today if it is not a good one, if it is not actually as good or superior to its competition. The truth of the matter is that the handicapped themselves have been the best sales entrepreneurs for their own employment, as is so remarkably set down on the following pages.

Jennings Randolph

United States Senator

Preface

In writing this book, I did not intend for it to be an autobiographic sketch of my life and work. Its purpose is to set forth the step-by-step activities which led to the passage of the Randolph-Sheppard Act and to point out the economic accomplishments of thousands of blind persons as the result of this legislation. At the same time, it is to serve as an education to the general public as to what blind persons can do from an economic standpoint if given a chance to do so. I also hope it will inspire many blind persons to seek rehabilitation counseling so that their lives of inactivity can become useful, not only to themselves and to their immediate families, but to their respective communities as well.

In writing the historic development of the legislation, I could not refrain from writing about some of the unpleasant events which took place along the path of the legislative battle. I am happy to be able to report that when there is an important piece of legislation before Congress today which is beneficial to blind persons, it has the unanimous support of every important organization for the blind and of the blind. In unity there is strength of purpose and greatness of accomplishment.

Leonard A. Robinson

Chapter 1

The World of Darkness

Being the youngest of five children, and the only one born in Knoxville, Tennessee, I remember my early childhood with my brother and sisters as being happy and joyous. My father was in the mercantile business just off the main street. He was a very hard-working man whose aim in life was to provide his family with the better things of life which he himself never had. My mother was a kind and soft-hearted individual. She was always ready at a moment's notice to be at the bedside of a sick neighbor and doing whatever she could to be of assistance wherever necessary.

It was on an October morning in 1911, when I was seven years old, that my first eye accident occurred. School was out for the day, and I was watching the corner grocer perform his chores in the yard next to his store. A boyfriend, slightly older than me, aimed his BB rifle and the BB shot entered my left eye, coming within an inch of hitting my brain. The eye was removed the next day. The right eye was not affected, and I learned to pursue my daily activities with the use of one eye instead of two. I do not recall I was handicapped in any way. An artificial left eye restored the cosmetic effect. I continued my activities with my childhood friends, and life continued on in that happy and joyous vein.

At the age of eleven I was playing with one of my boyfriends when he picked up a rock and hit me just above the right eye. I noticed no loss of sight, but six months later the retina of the right eye became detached.

After two years of treatment in Knoxville with limited success, my eye doctor suggested I go to Baltimore where I could obtain the services of Dr. Harry Friedenwald, a well-known ophthalmologist. He was partly successful in reattaching the retina, but before it could properly heal, a cataract complicated matters. That meant another six months' stay in the Baltimore hospital, with hardly any success at all. When I was on the operating table for about the seventh time, Dr. Friedenwald as much as told me that he did not think this operation would be any more successful than the previous ones. He knew he could talk to me quite frankly. He asked me what I intended to do with myself, and I recall, while still on the operating table before he had started his surgery, I told him I would go back to school and eventually take up law. I told him I thought I could be of greater service to society as a lawyer, and that was what I wanted to do.

One week later while still in the hospital, I began to make my plans to complete my education. Someone told me about the Evergreen School in Baltimore which trained blind persons. When I went over to make inquiry as to my chances for further education, I was told that the school was only for blind veterans of World War I. But, I was introduced to Miss Amy K. Halfpenny, who was a teacher at the Evergreen School. She was a graduate of the school for the blind in West Philadelphia, which was known as the Pennsylvania Institution for the Instruction of the Blind. She told me about how nice it was and suggested I write a letter to O. H. Burritt, its superintendent, to arrange for admission. In about three weeks I heard from Mr. Burritt, advising me I could be admitted at any time. I was admitted on a Sunday morning in February 1922, just one month before my eighteenth birthday. I was received by Mr. Burritt. He asked me what I intended to take up in college following my graduation. When I told him I was interested in law, I recall that he was not very enthusiastic.

That first day at the school for the blind was quite an experience for me. I had the idea that school children in a school for the blind were sad and morose. I do not know what caused me to believe that. I do not recall that I felt that way. As it was almost lunch time when I finished my interview with Mr. Burritt, my friend, who accompanied me from Baltimore, was directed to the Senior Cottage where I would be domiciled. When we went into the cloister around which all the cottages are built, I heard the cheerful and gay voices of boys who were striding down the cloister walk and busily engaged in enthusiastic conversation. At Cottage C, the older boys were waiting for me, and after I had been shown my sleeping quarters and deposited my suitcase, I joined them in the living room to await lunch.

There was nothing sad about those boys. They got me in a corner and began telling me a lot of dirty jokes. I had a few for them, too, since my stay in the Baltimore hospital allowed me to visit with the patients, and I picked up some pretty keen stories, which they also enjoyed. My initiation with the gang was then complete.

When I was recommended by Miss Halfpenny to go to the school for the blind in Philadelphia, I did not know that there was a school for the blind in Tennessee. There are residential schools for the blind in almost every state of the Union. Where there is no such school, blind children are sent to neighboring states to attend the school for the blind there which is paid for by the board of education of their own state. In those states which have no residential school for the blind, there are special classes within the public school systems of such states where the blind child is educated along with the sighted. It is interesting to note, however, that there are more blind children attending public schools in the United States than those who attend residential schools for the blind.

3

In work for the blind, professional workers seem to differ on which type of schooling is best for blind children. The residential segregated school, as it is referred to by some, is the classic center for the education of such children. There they receive all of their instruction. They go home only for weekends.

The public school arrangement, where the blind child attends school along with his fellow sighted classmates, is scheduled so that during certain intervals during the day he goes to what is called a "resource room" or "special aids center." Here an expert teacher furnishes him with the special learning devices he needs, including braille. This is also referred to as the "integrated braille class system."

Those who favor the residential school contend that the blind child can learn more rapidly where the educational system is devoted entirely to the blind. In such schools arrangements can be made for his musical education. Here there is vocal training, piano instruction, and instruction with other musical instruments. He can also obtain a fully rounded course in physical education; for at all such schools, there is a fully equipped gymnasium. If he is athletically inclined, he can become a member of a wrestling team, track team, swimming team, or bowling team. All residential schools have swimming pools and other types of athletic accommodations.

Those who contend that a blind child should attend a public school in his neighborhood argue that he can more easily retain his sighted friends' companionship. They also contend that these blind children do not easily fall into bad habits known as "blindisms."

As all of my professional work in the field of vocational rehabilitation was done in the District of Columbia, I would always refer parents of preschool blind children to the Maryland School for the Blind, as the District of Columbia public school system was not effectively developed to accommodate the blind child. The District Board of Education had arrangements with the Maryland School for the Blind to educate their blind children.

At the Overbrook School my progress was very rapid. I had been out of school for almost six years, trying to regain my sight. My first big task was to learn to read and write braille.

Louis Braille, who lived in France between the years of 1809 and 1852, was a French teacher of the blind. His system of raised dot writing has enabled the sightless to read and write music and literature. Three years after his birth near Paris, Braille lost his sight through an accident. He learned rapidly and also became a fine organist. He studied at the Paris Institute for the Blind, and in 1828 became a teacher at the school. It was there that he invented the system of reading and writing which bears his name. The Braille System was demonstrated in Paris in 1854 at the Paris International Exposition where it was finally adopted. This was two years after Braille's death.

The Braille System consists of six dots, three on each side, or in two vertical columns. The different arrangements of dots, anywhere from one dot to five dots, make up the alphabet. Braille grade one and one-half consists of contractions, and there are some sixty-three different combinations of dots in this particular system. Grade two braille followed later with a system of more complicated contractions.

I learned to read braille very quickly. First I mastered the straight braille which has no contractions. All the words are spelled out letter for letter. I mastered this in about a week. When I was able to visualize each letter in my mind's eye, so to speak, and memorized them, I was ready to read a book. I recall my first book was *Little Shepherd of Kingdom Come*, and I was thrilled to be able to once again do my own reading. I recall staying awake until twelve o'clock each night to finish my book, and this new burst of interest sped me along all the more quickly with my mastery of braille. My day classes with my special grade teacher, Elwood Govan, prepared me for contracted braille grade one and one-half and once I mastered this, I was ready to be assigned to regular classes.

I entered what was the equivalent of the first year of high school about five weeks after I entered the school for the blind. It reminded me of my school days of several years back. It was not much different. We went to class prepared for our instruction for that day and each boy was called upon by the teacher to answer questions just as I had been accustomed to in the past. I began to realize that being without sight was merely an inconvenience and not a handicap.

I still kept in touch with Mr. Govan of the special grade, who filled me in on certain details with which I felt I needed his special attention. When June came, I arranged with him that I would study the first year of Latin at home during the summer, and if I mastered it, he would give me a test upon my return in the fall. If I passed it, I would receive credit for the course. I found Latin very easy and very interesting from an English point of view, and for the first time learned what English grammar was all about. I passed the test upon my return. The next summer I studied the first year of German and passed that test upon my return to school that fall. In this way I was able to complete all of my high school subjects that the institute required by February of 1924 with enough credits left over to be admitted to the final semester of the fourth year of high school at the West Philadelphia High School for Boys. Thus, I was graduated from the institute on June 17, 1924, and three days later from the West Philadelphia High School.

I recall quite vividly the day of my graduation from the institute. There were several other boys and four girls in that graduating class. Each one of us had plans for further education or training for employment, and all of us were filled with optimism of what the future held for us. We had been told by our superintendent, O. H. Burritt, that society was ready to receive the educated and skilled blind person as soon as we were ready to offer our services.

But little did we know of that World of Darkness which surrounded us. Being without sight and with very little contact, if any at all, with the business world, we had no idea of the frustrations and disappointments blind persons were encountering in the day-to-day struggle for a living. As for myself, my plan was to enter college and someday practice law.

From this account of my schooling it is obvious that I did not take much time out for other activities. Part of my required training was manual arts, such as chair caning, rug weaving, and related subjects.

The school had an excellent reputation for athletic sports, and while I participated in them merely as part of my physical education training, I did not take time out to make a team. The athletic field was across the street, and I recall the long cable that reached the one hundred yards, to which was attached a chain and handle used by the totally blind student when running the hundred-yard dash. I remember I ran it once in sixteen seconds. But some of our athletes could do it in a little over ten seconds.

The Pennsylvania Institution for the Instruction of the Blind was founded in Philadelphia by the Society of Friends, March 5, 1835. A house was soon provided and the services of Julius R. Friedlander as principal were secured. After many years in the downtown section of the city, the school was moved to Overbrook, a western suburb of Philadelphia, and in 1947 was renamed the Overbrook School for the Blind.

In the fall of 1924, I was admitted as a freshman at the University of Tennessee. I acquired the services of a reader, a second-year student who also was interested in law, and in order to catch up with him I took some extra courses and went to summer school. He and I were graduated in June of 1927 with a Bachelor of Arts degree with the first year of law completed. We took what was called the arts-law course which permitted us to substitute the first year of law for the fourth year of arts. During the second year of law, I made up my mind to practice law in Cleveland, Ohio, where my brother and a sister lived, and my final year of law was taken at the Western Reserve University Law School in Cleveland. I was graduated from there in June of 1929 and was admitted to the Ohio Bar in August of that year.

When I opened my law office in the fall of 1929, I started out with some corporation law clients who were recommended to me by members of my family who had had business dealings with them. I had a competent legal male secretary who did my reading and research. It was during those early days of my law practice that I met up with alert and competent blind men and women who had sought my advice with reference to their own employment problems. During my last year at law school I had met many of them at socials, but I had not become acquainted with their problems and disappointments. Now, I was beginning to understand the kind of world in which the blind lived. Their greatest handicap was not their lack of sight, but rather it was the misunderstanding employers had of the capabilities of blind persons. Helen Keller once wrote: "Not blindness, but the attitude of the seeing to the blind, is the hardest burden to bear."

As a matter of fact, almost all physically handicapped persons have far more skills and assets than are lost through their impairments. All that is needed to develop their remaining skills and capacities is physical restoration to the extent possible, counseling and guidance, training, and placement on the job in accordance with their training and past experiences.

The philosophy underlying the training and rehabilitation and placement of the physically handicapped did not become evident until June 1920, when the first Vocational Rehabilitation Act was put into operation for the civilian population of the United States. Congress had passed a similar law in

1918 for the disabled of World War I, and the successful administration of this law led to the one in 1920.

Organized efforts to provide economic opportunities for the blind of the United States date back to the establishment of a workshop for the adult blind in 1840 as a department of the Perkins Institution and the Massachusetts School for the Blind. In 1850 this workshop was separated from the school and established as a separately operated division of the institution. Towards the end of the nineteenth century, the recognition of the need to provide employment opportunities for the blind lent such impetus to the development of employment facilities for the blind in the form of special workshops that by 1947 there were 103 such workshops for the blind scattered throughout the country.

For the most part, these workshops for the blind were set up for the making of brooms, mops, brushes, chair caning, and rug weaving. Blind men and women were selected because of their ability to perform well with their hands. Their minds were alert and their production good. In the early 1930's such workshop workers earned about forty to fifty dollars a month, and with this income they were deprived of state grants or pensions which were given to the less fortunate blind for whom there was not enough work in the workshops, and who had to exist on an average of thirty-five dollars a month from such pensions.

Ohio was the first state to pass an act providing for such pensions in 1898. This was followed by Illinois in 1903; by Wisconsin in 1907; by Kansas in 1911; and Minnesota in 1913. By the end of 1934 twenty-four states had passed such legislation.

This was the situation that the adult blind found himself in when I began my law practice in the early part of 1930. Little did I know what the true situation was with respect to the attitude of the general public towards the blind. My law practice was suffering from this attitude, but as we were living in what was regarded as the worst economic depression

9

in our history, sometimes referred to as the Hoover Depression, I was unable to realize fully what was causing my own difficulties from an economic standpoint.

In retrospect, and looking back upon those years, I read with great interest and understanding from the book *Blindness and the Blind in the United States,* written by Dr. Harry Best and published in 1934. From the book the following quotation is from "Reconstruction of Perkins Institution Pressing Need," in 1907 by Dr. E. E. Allen:

> The tragedy of blindness is not inability to see; it is the dread of dependence; of poverty and want and the pauper's grave. Childhood looks not far ahead; but young men and women, however cheerful they may generally appear, too often yield to periods of depression. It is but natural that the outlook should be dark and foreboding. The wonder is that this is so often and so readily relieved. Blindness borrows trouble; its victims are overcome by self-pity. Too frequently there follows a sinking of the fires of life, a flagging of energy resulting in idleness, morbidity, and ennui. Any people so oppressed in mind tend to deteriorate in every way—even morally.

Quoting further from Dr. Best, under the chapter entitled "Popular Conceptions Regarding Blind," the following is of interest:

> The position of the blind in society is further to be indicated by the conceptions which are held regarding them by their fellow men, or by the attitude entertained towards them by the community in general. Respecting the blind many erroneous conceptions, or misconceptions, are found to be cherished, which show little sign of abatement with the course of time. They are probably due primarily to the impression that in the loss of the sense of vision such a transcending change has been effected in one's composition and temperament as to remove one from the currents of ordinary life and ways. As few are called upon to associate intimately with the blind, there is often little chance of the realization of the true situation.
>
> The sentiment instantly excited at the sight of the blind is one of overwhelming pity for their condition. On nearly every hand manifestations of this compassion are to be found, awakened by a state that suggests helplessness, and invites help. When occasion

arises for its practical expression in some form of assistance, rarely is reluctance or hesitation displayed, but rather abundant willingness, and even eagerness. Though the method adopted to hold out a hand to the blind is not in every case, especially in such as involves the extension of material relief, a wisely chosen one, this seldom results from a want of concern in them or of a genuine desire to aid or serve them. Generous as are the motives of the public in respect to the blind, however, and creditable as are the acts of those who have had a part in succoring them, there does not always issue a complete understanding of the situation of the blind, nor is there prevented the rise of certain misapprehensions regarding them. . . .

Because of the great misunderstanding on the part of the general public towards the blind, very few blind persons during the first part of the twentieth century were able to find remunerative employment in our factories. Only in a few instances were the lucky among the blind engaged in factory or industrial work. Many of them received less pay for their labor than did their fellow sighted workers.

Quoting from Dr. Best, he says:

With many employers there is also a conviction that the blind are of necessity greatly lacking in the alacrity and celerity of movement to be expected of ordinary persons, perhaps merely plodding along in their work, and perhaps causing a slowing up generally of industrial operations—with productivity and output not inconsiderably reduced in consequence. The increasing use of machinery and of labor-saving devices in industry militates against them, and makes matters the worse for them. If, moreover, there is a scarcity of jobs among industrial workers in general, or if there is increased competition among them, it is the blind who will early feel the effects, and whose opportunities will be correspondingly diminished. . . .

This dark and dismal picture which partly describes the situation of the blind during the first few decades of this century and the general misunderstanding of them by the public, required a firm and vigorous national effort to do something constructive on their behalf.

11

Chapter 2

The Well in the Desert

There are many monthly braille magazines of current events and news of special interest to the blind. In 1931 one of these magazines was the *Braille Mirror* which was published by the Braille Institute of America in Los Angeles. In the March 1931 edition, there was a five-page article and editorial written by the institute's founder, J. Robert Atkinson, which told about a bill in Congress sponsored by Senator Thomas D. Schall of Minnesota, himself without sight. The bill had been introduced by Senator Schall in 1929. It authorized the establishment of news, candy, and refreshment stands in Federal buildings throughout the country to be operated by blind persons. A Bureau for the Blind was to be set up in the Department of Labor for the purpose of supervising the program.

Mr. Atkinson's editorial went on to explain the practicability of the proposed legislation from the standpoint of giving blind persons in such public places an opportunity to demonstrate that the blind can perform responsible tasks if given an opportunity to do so. But, as Mr. Atkinson pointed out, Senator Schall was not getting anywhere with the bill as he was not receiving any support from organized agencies for the blind, including the American Foundation for the Blind of New York City.* To them the bill was unimportant and

*The American Foundation for the Blind, under the distinguished leadership of Dr. M. Robert Barnett, executive director, has rendered a distinct and valuable service during the past twenty-five years in the area of research and program activity designed to improve services to blind persons of all ages.

deserved no support. As I was not a professional worker for the blind, I could not understand the pros and cons of such a program, but I made up my mind I would find out.

The following month, in April 1931, there was to be a World Conference on Work for the Blind in New York City, to be sponsored by the American Foundation for the Blind. I attended that conference as a representative of the Cleveland Chapter of the Welfare Sightless Association. This association had a membership of some forty or fifty blind persons and partially sighted, all of whom were very much interested in the Schall Bill. If it became a law a few of them might be permanently rehabilitated as a result of it. The two or three Federal buildings in Cleveland could pave the way for other similar vending stands to be opened on behalf of the blind in the county and city buildings.

At one of the morning sessions of the World Conference which I attended, the name of Joseph F. Clunk was announced. He was representing the Canadian National Institute for the Blind of Toronto, Canada, and his talk that morning was on the employment of blind persons in Canada. Almost all of his subject dealt with the vending stand program in Federal buildings in Canada to which blind persons were assigned as operators. I had never heard of Mr. Clunk, but from that moment on, he and I became very close friends. When he had finished with his talk, I went to him on the platform and told him my reason for being at the conference. I told him he had convinced me that such a project for the blind was very practical.

Mr. Clunk in his speech had pointed out how the blind stand operators were trained and how efficiently they were operating their stands. He stated that the institute was constantly besieged with calls from industrialists who wanted to give space in their establishments for vending stands to be run by blind persons. He spoke of the importance in such a program to have vending stand equipment made up specially for each location, and that such equipment should be of excellent quality. He stressed the importance of "good house-keeping," pointing out that badly maintained stands and stocks of merchandise were distractions to a stand program based on efficient business operation. The vending stand program in Canada, as Mr. Clunk pointed out, was known as a supervised controlled operation. No stand ever became the sole property of the blind stand operator. His business operations were under constant supervision by trained professional personnel of the institute, and the more successful stand operators who could take on larger responsibilities were transferred to larger stands which meant more net profit to them.

I told Mr. Clunk about the article I had read in the *Braille Mirror* just the month before, concerning the vending stand bill in Congress and the opposition to it. He assured me that we could do a better job in the United States than they were doing in Canada with such a program as the distances between some of the stands in Canada were quite long. He pointed out that a state like Pennsylvania could easily have several hundred stands. The supervision of the stands would be quite simple in such a state, where the locations could be within easy reach. And then he emphasized what a program like this could be in each of our then forty-eight states. He promised to write letters to anyone I suggested which might help the Schall Bill become a law, and with that promise, I told him I would go to Washington from New York to see Senator Schall before I returned to Cleveland.

When I told Mr. Clunk that I lived in Cleveland, he told me that he, too, had lived there and that he had lost his sight while in Cleveland. I later found out that he became blind just before his first child was born. He was twenty-one years of age at the time. With the greater responsibility facing him, he had no time to grieve over the total loss of sight, and when his doctor told him that nothing could be done for him, he bought a white cane and learned to travel by himself. In those days there were no mobility instructors for the blind as

14

there are now. He became a door-to-door salesman and earned a living, but in a difficult way.

It was not long before Mr. Clunk realized what the blind were up against insofar as earning a living was concerned. He had met other blind persons in Cleveland who had potential industrial skills, but who needed training and assistance in getting placed on the job.

The Cleveland Society for the Blind was looking for someone who might be helpful in finding employment for blind persons, and Mr. Clunk was hired for the job. What I would call a miraculous sense seemed to develop for Mr. Clunk, as he had no difficulty finding industrial processes that required no sight and which blind persons could perform on a par with sighted persons. He would seek the cooperation of a factory foreman or superintendent who would let him go through the factory with one of them to discover such processes. They would describe each operation to him, and if he felt that he could do it, he took off his coat and would demonstrate right then and there that he, a totally blind person, could perform that process and without getting his fingers caught in the machines. In this way, Clunk placed many blind persons of Cleveland in factory jobs. He would accompany them to the job, explain the processes, and train the blind persons at their machines. The placement was not final until the foreman assured Mr. Clunk that the new blind employee was working out satisfactorily.

When Mr. Clunk went to Canada, the idea of vending stands being operated by blind persons was not new so far as he was concerned. This is borne out in a speech which he gave in 1958 before a conference of workers for the blind in which he stated:

> The present day concept of vending stands is reputed to have started about 1895, and it is quite likely that blind persons operated sizable retail businesses in this country long before that. It so happens that I am old enough to remember that about 1920 blind persons were establishing themselves, or were established by their

15

friends, in the industrial plants of Ohio, Michigan, and New England, where they ran lunch services of one kind or another. In 1919, when I came into the field of work, the refreshment stand in an industrial plant or in an office building, operated by a blind person, was already one of the accepted methods of employment. However, the installations were widely scattered, and, because of the almost universal installation of poor equipment and of inadequate stocks . . . failed as rapidly as they were installed. . . .

When the Youngstown Association for the Blind was established, about 1925, Mr. Clunk was hired to direct its activities. As this was steel mill country and other types of related factories were nearby, Clunk had no difficulty in obtaining employment for blind persons residing in the Youngstown area.

In 1928 the Canadian National Institute for the Blind was interested in opening up an employment placement for the blind. Mr. Clunk heard about the opening and applied for the job. It was then and there that he thought of vending stands for the blind, and that program became his foremost objective at the outset. He was so successful with that part of the program that getting jobs for other blind persons in industries in Canada became a sideline, but a very successful one.

Joseph F. Clunk, because of his tremendous record on behalf of the employable blind, was that silver lining in those dark clouds for the blind of Canada which was destined to shed its light also on behalf of the blind of the United States. The Schall Bill and Mr. Clunk's accomplishments became that well in the desert which never dried up.

Having had several conferences with Mr. Clunk at the World Conference, and learning from him the way he went about his work, I knew I would bring good tidings to Senator Schall when I reached Washington. Fortunately, the senator was in town and was able to give me as much time as I wanted. I told him all about the Canadian program and about Mr. Clunk, and I assured him that his bill for the blind was practical and sound. He made it clear that without help from those in work for the blind he could not do much with it. He had introduced the bill at the suggestion of another blind person who was not in a position to be of help.

Senator Schall impressed me as a man who was vitally interested in doing something constructive for other blind persons. He, himself, had made a very good adjustment to blindness. He was well aware of the difficulties blind persons were having in finding suitable employment. He assured me that his office was ready to do anything and everything to bring about the passage of his legislation, and he told me that I was at liberty to use his office anytime that I was in Washington.

As Mr. Clunk promised, he wrote me a letter in which he described his employment program for the blind in Canada, including industrial placement of blind persons and the vending stand program. The letter read as follows:

I understand that you are interested in the history of placement work in Canada, and the following information may be of some value to you.

The Canadian National Institute for the Blind is a national organization expending an annual budget of approximately $375,000 a year for all services in all parts of the Dominion. Fifty percent of this budget is raised from government sources, such as Provincial, municipal, county, and Federal. The remainder is raised by private contributions. The organization is managed by a board of directors, is not political in any sense of the word, and is not subject to political intervention. Its activities include all of the services rendered in the United States—National, State, and city organizations, libraries, printing houses, prevention of blindness services, and homes, and thus includes every service to blind persons except the operation of schools for children.

The placement department is the youngest branch of the service and started its work May 1, 1928, with one staff worker. Placements have been made in many types of industry, and approximately 50 different industries have been surveyed and practical processes revealed. These processes include such work as operating drill presses, tapping machines, bolt threaders, light punch presses, milling machines, candy dipping or enrobing machines, assembly of small parts, delivery from circular saws and printing presses in wood box factories, stuffing cushions in automobile plants, wrapping candy bars, repairing cases in breweries, stringing tennis racquets, etc.

Owing to the fact that during the last three or four years production processes have not been available because of factory closedowns we have gone into the management of industrial lunch stands. These opportunities are planned for and are used by blind persons who would not ordinarily be employed in manual occupations because of age or lack of mechanical ability. In some cases, where the individual might have sufficient mechanical ability he has too much personality and business talent to justify burial of his energy in a factory-production process. At the present time we operate more than 150 of these stands across the Dominion. They are located in some of the largest industrial plants, in Provincial and city buildings, in hospitals such as the ordinary medical institution, as well as the mental hospitals, in universities, and in small communities we operate small stores located on city property with a sidewalk frontage. We have evolved a system of management which brings in a return from the stands to our organization to cover a portion of the cost of repairs, insurance, depreciation, and supervision.

This system also provides a weekly drawing account for the blind person and a net profit check for the actual earnings of the business every four weeks. The results have been most satisfactory and we are in the happy position of possessing a public opinion which is now bringing us in invitations from large companies to operate their industrial cafeteria services, and in some cases these companies pay us a subsidy in order to make the business a practical one for us. . . . It is not unusual for us to find ourselves short of good material in the field of blind persons for the available opportunities.

Our system is not duplicated anywhere and so far as we know it is entirely original, and is based upon six years of intensive experience and the expenditure of approximately $150,000 for development. We now believe that we have a system of operating stands which will make that part of our work self-supporting, which will develop a positive public opinion and which will create more opportunities than we require in this field of effort.

Our placement staff at the present time consists of two placement agents in Ontario, two aftercare workers, who supervise housekeeping, menu, training, etc., a full-time and a part-time bookkeeping supervisor. In the Provinces of Manitoba and Saskatchewan we have one full-time placement agent. In the Prov-

inces of British Columbia and Alberta we have one full-time placement agent. In the Province of Quebec we have one full-time
aftercare worker and impetus is given to the sales effort from the
Ontario staff. In the maritime Provinces of Nova Scotia, New
Brunswick, and Prince Edward Island we have one aftercare supervisor.

During the past month, in Ontario, we have opened four business opportunities and each of them has been at the invitation of
the company with whom we are associated. One is located in a
gold mine, 450 miles north of Toronto. The second is in a high
school, 225 miles east of Toronto. The other two are in large
industrial concerns in the city. We know that our system can be
adopted by city and State organizations and that it is even more
workable in your densely populated country than it is here where
our distances are so great and our population so scattered. . . .

It was quite obvious that Mr. Clunk intended his letter to
influence the skeptical worker in the field of work for the
blind and at the same time to educate those members of
Congress who might be influenced to work for the passage of
a suitable vending stand bill if they had knowledge of its
practicability. I sent copies of it to Mr. Atkinson in Los
Angeles and to Senator Schall, who were encouraged and delighted with its contents.

During the remainder of 1931 and the early part of 1932 I
was in correspondence with certain workers for the blind
who did manifest an interest in the vending stand legislation.
I was not sure then what role, if any, I would play in its
passage. I still had my law practice to worry about. I was
unmarried at the time and resided with my mother and sister.

Some of the replies to the letters I sent out were very
discouraging. I recall one of them written by a professional
worker for the blind stated that the vending stand bill was
unconstitutional. This did not seem to worry me at the time.
I reasoned that those engaged in the field of work for the
blind would never contest its constitutionality in any court
of law, and after it once became a law and was in operation,

19

no one or any group of persons would be so low as to deprive a blind person of his livelihood.

After giving the matter of constitutionality some thought, I decided to write to my law professor who taught me my course in constitution law at the Western Reserve University Law School. He was Archibald Throckmorton who wrote the section dealing with Constitution Law for Corpus Juris, which was considered the lawyer's best reference source. In my letter to Mr. Throckmorton I pointed out the need and the practicability of the pending bill in Congress pertaining to the vending stand authorization in Federal buildings for the benefit of blind persons. Soon thereafter I received a reply to my letter which was very brief and to the point. Mr. Throckmorton contended that there was nothing unconstitutional about the legislation since the Federal Government could do anything it wished with its Federal buildings.

Another letter I received contended that the vending bill legislation would have no chance of passage in Congress since it would be opposed by the various veterans' organizations who were interested in the blind of World War I. I decided I would cross that bridge when I got to it.

At the World Conference on Work for the Blind I met Representative Matthew A. Dunn of Pittsburgh, who was also totally without sight and was a member of the Pennsylvania legislature. Mr. Dunn also liked the idea of the Schall Bill. He told me then that he had given some thought to running for Congress in 1932, and if nothing happened to the Schall Bill, and if he was successful in his congressional campaign, he would be glad to see what he could do with such a bill.

Chapter 3

Campaign for Legislation Begins

Upon my return from Washington where I was in conference with Senator Schall, I wrote to Mr. Atkinson in Los Angeles, telling him of my meeting with Mr. Clunk at the World Conference on Work for the Blind in New York City and the endorsement Mr. Clunk gave of the legislation. I realized that my efforts in behalf of the vending stand legislation could best be accomplished by my close contact with Mr. Atkinson. When he received a copy of Mr. Clunk's letter in connection with the Canadian program, he advised me to whom to write for their cooperation in connection with the Schall Bill. These persons Mr. Atkinson recommended were well known in the professional field of work for the blind, and my purpose was to acquaint them with the legislation and to get their support for it. As pointed out in Chapter 2, some of these replies were discouraging. By this time I had made up my mind that I would begin a national campaign to get support for the legislation, and with Mr. Clunk's promise to write letters to important persons in Congress with respect to it, I felt I had sufficient support to get an active campaign started.

Early in 1932 when the political picture in the country looked in the direction of Governor Franklin D. Roosevelt to be the Democratic presidential nominee, I made up my mind that I would actively campaign for him in Ohio, and to that end, I contacted one of my Cleveland congressmen, Martin L.

Sweeney, and my Democratic senator, Robert J. Bulkley, and obtained their interest in my active campaign work in the presidential election. They were also very much in favor of the legislation benefiting the blind which Senator Schall was sponsoring, and I realized that their interest and active support of the legislation would be very helpful.

The State Democratic Committee in Ohio arranged for me to speak at various places within Ohio, and my assignment was to represent the presidential candidate and those running for Congress in their respective communities. My first speaking engagement was near the city of Warren.

On November 4, 1932, I sent the following letter to Governor Franklin D. Roosevelt:

Cleveland, Ohio
November 4, 1932

Hon. Franklin D. Roosevelt,
Governor of New York,
Albany, N. Y.

Dear Governor Roosevelt:

As one of the workers in the "Ohio for Roosevelt" movement, I feel it is safe to say at this late date in the campaign that Ohio will go Democratic by at least two hundred thousand. I believe I express the sentiments of the Democratic workers throughout the country that our aim is to obtain for you not only the Presidency, but also a majority of the popular vote as well as the electoral vote such as will never be forgotten during our lifetime. I believe that almost everyone realizes that a new day in our political history has arrived, and that a new leader with liberal views and policies must navigate the ship of destiny to safer and quieter waters. It is my hope, as well as my prediction, that twenty-five million Americans will choose you as the Captain of the Ship of State. May I also add here that it is my sincere hope that you will receive an electoral vote in excess of 444.

It was my pleasure and privilege to address a few hundred persons, most of whom were Republicans, in a strong Republican section in Ohio. Only two or three Democrats have held important offices in the entire history of the county. This Democratic rally took place in a small township, and the school auditorium was filled to capacity by persons living in the vicinity and adjoin-

22

ing towns. Their enthusiastic welcome given me and the other speakers on the program and their appreciative response to our messages reflected only too well their sentiments and their distrust in the present order of things. The enclosed clipping which appeared in "Warren Tribune Chronicle"—a Republican newspaper—might be of interest to you.

My interest during the past twelve years has been in work for the blind. Being without sight myself, it is only natural that I should be interested in this most complicated part of social service work. The man without sight has been not only the forgotten man but the unknown man. It has always been my contention that the sightless man's handicap is not the fact that he has no sight but rather the fact that he is not understood by his fellowmen and by society generally. There has been a bill in Congress during the past two sessions designed to benefit the blind without the Government having to go to any expense. If this bill becomes a law and if its details are carried out to the fullest extent, the problems of the blind will be virtually solved. Judge Martin L. Sweeney and Senator Robert J. Bulkley are willing to do whatever they can to bring about the passage of this bill, and, as I mentioned to Judge Sweeney not long ago, it is my desire that you sign the bill rather than have the present administration get credit for it. Some of your closest friends here in Cleveland as well as in upper New York State suggest my going to Albany some time after the election to discuss this matter with you.

I wish you continued success and an overwhelming victory, and remain

Respectfully yours,

(Signed)   Leonard A. Robinson

On November 18, President-elect Roosevelt sent me the following letter:

Nov. 18, 1932.

Mr. Leonard A. Robinson,
1110 Hippodrome Building,
Cleveland, Ohio.

My dear Mr. Robinson:

It was fine to read your letter of November 4th which just reached my desk today. I want you to know that I appreciate the efforts of yourself and my other friends in Ohio who helped to bring about a wonderful victory on November 8th.

If there is nothing done about the bill you referred to during the coming session of Congress and if Senator Robert J. Bulkley will bring this to my attention some time after the 4th of next March, I will be very glad to give it my careful consideration.

Thanking you for your good wishes, I am

Yours very sincerely,

Franklin D. Roosevelt

24

I was certainly elated when I received the letter from President-elect Roosevelt. I was more determined than ever to obtain a conference with him some time before he was inaugurated on March 4. I realized that he would be very busy with far more important things than the legislation for the blind as this country was experiencing its worst economic depression. On the day he was inaugurated every bank in the country was closed because of this economic condition, awaiting such legislation that a special Congress would enact to get the country back on its economic feet again.

I prevailed upon Congressman Sweeney and Senator Bulkley to arrange this conference for me with the President-elect, and after much correspondence between Albany and their respective offices, I received the following letter from Miss Le Hand:

EXECUTIVE MANSION

Albany, New York

December 29, 1932

Leonard A. Robinson, Esq.,
1110 Hippodrome Building,
Cleveland, Ohio.

My dear Mr. Robinson:

The Governor has asked me to tell you that he will be delighted to see you at his home 49 East 65th Street, New York City, on Friday, January sixth at eleven-thirty in the morning.

Very sincerely yours,

(Signed)   M. A. Le Hand

Private Secretary.

I arrived at Mr. Roosevelt's New York City home in time for my appointment on January 6. I did not get in to see him until some time after twelve-thirty. He was quite busy with many callers who had come to see him about the pressing problems of the day, and many of them were members of Congress. I was accompanied on this occasion by a close New York City friend of mine, David Stein. I recall that when we were ushered into the room where Mr. Roosevelt was seated, we were directed by Mr. Roosevelt to sit in certain chairs which had already been arranged and which were to one side of the chair in which he was seated. I did not know why he was so careful to point all this out to us, but soon we were seated and our conference was under way.

My first surprise and great pleasure was the realization that he knew for what purpose we had come, and he immediately told me that he thought the vending stand bill for the blind in which I was interested was a very practical project for blind persons. He told me that while Governor he had signed an executive order granting permission to two blind persons to operate such stands in two of the state buildings in Albany. I told him that I did not know about this, and I was glad to hear him say that these two blind persons were very successful in the operation of such stands. He promised that he would approve such legislation after his inauguration on March 4 if the pending legislation was not enacted by then. He extended an invitation to me to see him some time after the inauguration. To say that I was the happiest person in the world at that moment would be a gross understatement.

When my friend and I reached the outside of his house, the first thing I asked him was why Mr. Roosevelt was so careful in pointing out just where we were to sit. Mr. Stein replied: "Didn't you know there was a beautiful redhead painting his portrait?" I told him I did not hear her move, and besides my interest was so much taken up with my conversation with Mr. Roosevelt that I would not have heard anything anyway. A few weeks later Mr. Stein sent me a clipping taken from one of the New York City papers showing this artist at work with Mr. Roosevelt seated at his desk. The artist was Natalie van Vleck.

Another thing which impressed me concerning this conference with Mr. Roosevelt was his tremendous knowledge of the subject I came to see him about. I recall reading in some of my braille books during the months preceding this conference that certain persons would call on the President-elect for the purpose of giving him ideas about certain things that they believed he was not familiar with and which would be of great interest to the well-being of the country. They would come away astonished at the realization that Mr. Roosevelt knew more about the subject than they did. Well, this was exactly what I had experienced myself. I had never seen a blind person operating a vending stand. He had.

In April of 1933 I went to the White House to see the President, just as he had suggested. I was ushered into the office of his appointment secretary, Marvin McIntyre, who came out with a notation from the President informing me that an executive order would be signed, authorizing blind persons to sell newspapers and magazines inside Federal buildings, and that the Secretary of the Treasury, Mr. Woodin, would be in charge of the matter. Mr. McIntyre suggested that I go over and have a talk with Secretary Woodin and he set up the appointment for me.

A few days later I kept my appointment with Secretary Woodin, who received me very graciously. He read to me the executive order which would be put into operation and I told him my frank opinion of it. I made it very clear that no blind person could earn an adequate living selling only newspapers and magazines inside Federal buildings, and that the only solution to the problem was to have Congress pass such legislation that would give supervisory control by some Federal government agency over such a project, such as the Schall Bill provided for. I pointed out since this was a nationwide project, and since such a program could succeed only with the cooperation of agencies for the blind in every state, that national legislation was the only solution. I told him about the program in Canada and how it was carried out. I made it very clear that the executive order could remain in force until Congress got around to enacting the legislation in question. I also told him I did not think many blind persons would avail themselves of the executive order provision.

Three months later the executive order was rescinded. I do

27

not know what brought this about, but by then I was so engrossed in another bill before Congress that I did not take time to find out what actually happened.

Chapter 4

The Dunn Bill

Representative Matthew A. Dunn, whom I met while attending the World Conference on Work for the Blind in New York City, had now become a member of Congress. He was elected in November 1932. During my visits to Washington in April and June of 1933 I had been in conference with him concerning the vending stand legislation, and he was still very much interested in it. Since there seemed to be some opposition to such legislation by the Post Office Department, we decided to write a new bill which was known as the Dunn Bill, and in this one we authorized that a Bureau for the Blind be set up in the Post Office Department which could easily supervise such a project if the bill were enacted into law. It was during this time that the Treasury Department was transferring all of the Federal buildings under its jurisdiction to the Post Office Department.

On May 19, 1933, Congressman Dunn introduced his bill in the House of Representatives designated as H.R. 5694, "A bill to create a Bureau of the Blind in the Post Office Department, to provide for the issuing of licenses to blind persons to operate stands in Federal buildings, and for other purposes."

After the introduction of this bill, I had many conferences with various high officials of the Post Office Department, including Silliman Evans, first assistant postmaster general, and S. W. Purdum, fourth assistant postmaster general. Mr.

Evans did not voice any real objection to such legislation. He was very courteous to me. I had taken the opportunity to acquaint him with my visit to New York City to meet with President-elect Roosevelt and how he was in favor of such legislation. Most of my conferences were with Mr. Purdum as he was in charge of the buildings under the jurisdiction of the Post Office Department. Mr. Purdum, I recall, was inclined to doubt whether the blind could operate vending stands in any building, for that matter. I think he was quite impressed with the practicability of the Canadian program after reading the account of it so well explained in Mr. Clunk's letter to me.

It was evident that the Dunn Bill needed the full support of agencies for the blind located in all sections of the United States, and most of my time was spent on acquainting such agencies with it. Mr. Atkinson through his various publications was helpful in getting the message across.

In December of 1933 I was advised that a hearing on the Dunn Bill would take place in February of 1934. I prevailed upon the American Foundation for the Blind to call a conference in New York City some time in late December to discuss the merits of the legislation, and such a conference did take place. This was attended by some eight or ten persons representing agencies for the blind. I represented my Cleveland group known as the Cleveland Chapter of the Welfare Sightless Association.

I made it clear that if we all worked together towards the passage of the Dunn Bill we could easily get it through Congress since President Roosevelt had endorsed the idea to me personally. Everyone at the conference was aware of my contact with Mr. Roosevelt at his New York City home.

The conference lasted for several hours. There was not a great deal of enthusiasm exhibited. There were doubts that such an idea could ever be passed by Congress due to the skepticism on the part of the general public as to the ability of blind persons. I remember that my strongest point was that if the bill ever passed Congress, it would be a real demonstration of what blind persons could really do, and that this would be the finest object lesson we could bring about so far as the general public was concerned.

When the meeting was drawing to a close in the late afternoon, a suggestion was made that there would be an effort made by agencies for the blind to try to get through a presidential executive order and thus create the same thing that the bill would do. I reminded them of the executive order signed by Secretary Woodin several months past and how it came to an end by one simple stroke of the pen. My contention was that if Congress enacted this legislation and it became a law, it would take another act of Congress to repeal it, and I could never visualize Congress taking away thousands of such opportunities from blind persons all over the country. I further made it clear that the association I represented would never go along with an executive order and that we would not spend our time or money on such a project. The final suggestion was that if the executive order idea was not possible, then efforts would be made to get the legislation passed. I told them that all of my efforts would be in favor of the legislation.

On February 14, 1934, a hearing took place on H.R. 5694, the Dunn Bill, and according to the public record of this hearing, not one person who was at that New York City meeting participated at this hearing except me.

Mr. Atkinson, with whom I kept in close touch at all times, was also opposed to a presidential executive order. The following telegram was sent by Mr. Atkinson to Chairman James Mead of the Committee on Post Offices and Post Roads, Home Office Building:

> Braille Institute of America and Bureau of Social Welfare and Better Business for Blind endorse legislation proposed in Dunn Bill giving stand concessions in Federal buildings to blind licensees. As Editor of three magazines for blind and Founder of National Institution for Advancement of Blind, can show why legislation is more satisfactory than Presidential Executive order

31

plan being advocated. Sorry notice of hearing came too late to attend personally.

Attending the Dunn Bill hearing with me was Glen H. Hoffman, representing the Welfare Sightless Association of Ohio. The text of his statement reads as follows:

I represent the Welfare Association of Sightless of Ohio. The point I wanted to cover was the one with reference to the possible economy of the act referred to.

I will illustrate what I wish to make clear by my own community, because I happen to be more familiar there than with the entire country; however, I think the illustration will fit the entire country.

In Cuyahoga County we have 700 blind people. Of the 700, 290 are below school age; but, of course, are charges upon their parents. Three hundred others are persons who are otherwise handicapped, in addition to being blind—persons who have lost their sight when past middle age and could not under any circumstances fill such an opportunity. That leaves you with 120 of that group of 700 who could, if given the opportunity, take advantage of such a law.

Now, this approximate number has been schooled in the Ohio State School for the Blind, or in the sight-saving classes there in the public schools, and it has cost the community a considerable sum of money in order to give them education; and they have been told and taught, all during their education, just as I was myself, that when they had obtained the education they could go out and function in the world the same as sighted people.

Now, naturally, to walk out of school with your glories won, especially under a handicap, as we have had to get our education, and then to find that the doors of employment are closed to you, is a very bitter disappointment.

Now, going back to the economic issue of the thing, if you turn these pupils out and then do not employ them, you have not only lost what you paid for their education but you have thrown them on the community, which, according to the poorhouse funds of our community, would cost you at the lowest, under these conditions, $400 a year to keep them. Now, at $400 a year, 120 persons will cost you $48,000. I am speaking of Cuyahoga County alone. Now, all we ask for here is a measure whereby you open the opportunity to give those 120 people respectable employment from which they can earn a livelihood to support themselves and possibly any dependents that they might have; and in Cuyahoga County, or in whatever community they may have lived in, in addition to having given them the opportunity to live like other citizens, after all, you have not only given them an opportunity to live but you have actually taken a burden from the county taxes of that particular community.

Now, that percentage will hold good all through the United States, and that constitutes about one fifth. So that if you can employ that one fifth, you have employed all that you can possibly employ. And I believe there are enough opportunities in the United States to take care of one fifth. If there are, then you have taken off of the poor funds of the United States just one fifth of the burden they now have, or would have to carry under any circumstances.

The Dunn Bill did not pass. I do not recall it ever being acted upon by the committee.

Chapter 5

Creation of Cleveland Committee
for the Legislation

Soon after the public hearing on the Dunn Bill, H.R. 5694, which took place in February 1934, I realized that it was necessary to create a committee in Cleveland which could be organized to obtain support from every section of the country for the vending stand legislation. Outside of the District of Columbia, no person representing an organization for the blind testified, with the exception of Glen H. Hoffman, who came from Cleveland, representing the Welfare Sightless Association.

My friends who were members of the Cleveland Chapter of the Welfare Sightless Association agreed that a committee should be formed whose purpose would be to obtain national support for the vending stand legislation. We agreed that the committee be called Citizens Welfare Sightless Committee.

The next thing of importance was to obtain the services of a person who would serve as chairman of the committee. I took my case before the Cleveland Ministerial Committee, and when I had finished with my talk, I was introduced to Dr. Dan F. Bradley, pastor of the Pilgrim Congregational Church of West Cleveland. Dr. Bradley, who was around seventy years of age at the time, was noted as "Dean" of the ministers of Ohio, as he was beloved and respected by everyone who knew him. Dr. Bradley impressed me at the very beginning as he told me he was interested in all Federal legislation. He read the *Congressional Record* and kept up with all important legislation which affected individuals. He agreed to serve as overall chairman of the committee and I served as its executive chairman. The committee from that time on was in business.

My first step was to get newspaper endorsements from every section of the country. I contacted the Washington *Times* in the District of Columbia, which was a part of the Hearst syndicate, and obtained their immediate support for the legislation. This was an afternoon paper, and their morning edition was the Washington *Herald.* I recall quite vividly how Michael J. Flynn, managing editor of the *Herald,* would tell me to submit articles from time to time with respect to the progress of the legislation, and he would insert the articles pretty much the way I submitted them.

On one of my very frequent trips to Washington, I called upon the city editor of the Washington *Daily News.* He introduced me to one of the top executives of the Scripps-Howard syndicate. I do not recall his name, but I do remember that I obtained an immediate endorsement of the legislation which set into motion favorable articles and editorials in Scripps-Howard newspapers in every section of the country. In Cleveland it was the Cleveland *Press.* Louis B. Selzer was the managing editor of this newspaper and I was always welcome to call at the city desk any time I had anything new or of importance to report.

To obtain the support of the Paul Block syndicate, I drove over to Toledo, Ohio, and had a conference with the managing editor of the Toledo *Blade,* Grover Patterson. I recall how interested he was in the legislation. Of course in all of my interviews with the newspapermen, I took with me a copy of the letter I received from Mr. Clunk which told of the vending stand program in Canada, and this seemed to be enough evidence to these newspapermen that I was not trying to put through some kind of impractical project for the blind. I received copies of the editorials and news items from all these syndicates and used them whenever the occasion called for it.

In order to gain the support of organized labor, it was necessary for me to call upon the various labor organizations personally, just as I did with the newspaper syndicates. I was told about the Railway Labor Executives Association which had its national office in Washington. I recall when I first approached this organization I was introduced to Arthur J. Lovell, vice-president and national legislative representative of the Brotherhood of Locomotive Firemen and Enginemen. He became interested in my cause immediately and explained to me that the Railway Labor Executives Association was comprised of twenty-one railroad labor organizations with a total of approximately two million railroad employees. He told me he would take whatever steps necessary to obtain the endorsement of the overall railway association, and once that was obtained, he would be authorized to represent the association before any congressional committee on behalf of the vending stand legislation. His support was invaluable, as later chapters of this book will show.

I then approached the American Federation of Labor, whose Washington office at the time was located at Ninth and Massachusetts Avenue, N.W. The Congress of Industrial Organizations did not exist at that time. My contact was with the legislative committee of the federation, and there I met William C. Hushing. He was very sympathetic and under-standing, and he promised to spread the word around to the other legislative representatives concerning the vending stand legislation. He made it very clear, however, that his office could do nothing for the legislation without some official action taken on its behalf by the American Federation of Labor Executive Committee.

About five months after I had met with Mr. Hushing, the American Federation of Labor Executive Committee met in Cleveland. I was very fortunate to be able to obtain a personal meeting with William Green who was at that time president of the federation. I gave him the supporting material of the vending stand legislation I had at that time and he told me he would turn it over to some of the committee members for study, and if at all possible, he would try to get some action on behalf of the bill. About four weeks later I received a letter from Mr. Green advising me that the Executive Committee, when it met in Cleveland, endorsed the principle of the vending stand legislation. This was good news to me, and the next time I was in Washington I met with Mr. Hushing, who told me he knew of the action taken and that he was authorized, together with others of the Legislative Committee, to take whatever action was necessary to obtain favorable action on the legislation.

With the various newspapers already committed on behalf of the vending stand legislation, it was comparatively easy for me to obtain the endorsement of the American Newspaper Guild. This organization also met in Cleveland, and it was on the occasion of one of their national conventions that I was introduced to its president, Heywood C. Broun. I told him that I would like to speak for three or four minutes before their group to tell them personally what the vending stand legislation meant to the blind, and he consented to my request. I recall I was ushered in for this purpose, and when I was finished with my little talk, I thanked them for listening to me and excused myself and left. I did not want to answer any questions as I knew I had already exceeded my three or four minutes, but that was all that it took to get their endorsement of the legislation.

What I thought would be the most difficult of all to accomplish was the endorsement of the legislation by the various veterans' organizations. The American Legion national headquarters was located on K Street, N.W., in Washington, and I went to their headquarters to speak to their national legislative chairman. I do not recall his name, but he was very cooperative and understanding. He told me about a national

American Legion convention, which was going to take place in Saint Louis, and suggested that I go there and try to get before the convention with my story. I did as he suggested, but it was impossible for me to appear before the convention as the agenda had already been planned and they could not make room for me. Someone suggested that I get in touch with Captain Watson B. Miller, who was the chairman of the national legislative committee, and ask if I could speak before his group. I found Captain Miller a very friendly person and vitally interested in the legislation. I appeared before his committee and was given plenty of time to discuss the matter. Questions were asked, and it was apparent that they were very much interested. They realized that the vending stand legislation could benefit blinded veterans, and they did not single out the blinded veteran from the blinded civilian. To them there was no difference, for all blind persons seeking employment, whether veterans or non-veterans, needed this kind of employment opportunity. Some time later I obtained word that they would do whatever was necessary to help me with the legislation, but in an unofficial manner.

When I was in Washington again, I called at the offices of the Veterans of Foreign Wars, and the Disabled American Veterans, and explained to them the importance of the vending stand legislation to all blind persons. Both of these veterans' associations promised their full cooperation.

The important thing about the support I would be getting from these three veterans' groups was that they would not oppose the legislation because it did not give exclusive privilege to blind veterans. All of them took the attitude that what was good for one blind person was good for all of them who sought employment.

Chapter 6

Lions International Becomes Interested
in the Legislation

In June of 1934 I was in Washington again on one of my frequent visits to the Capitol City, conferring with Congressman Dunn to ascertain what chances the Dunn Bill had in getting favorable consideration by the House Post Office and Roads Committee. It was quite apparent that no action would be taken soon, and Congressman Dunn was not optimistic about it.

In my quest for organizations and group support for the legislation, I was advised to obtain the assistance of the Lions clubs since their major activity and interest were in the field of work for the blind. On all my trips to Washington I stayed at the Y.M.C.A. where my companion and I could obtain room accommodations at a very reasonable rate. Accompanying me on such trips was either one of my nephews or some young man who was out of work and who could handle my car efficiently and defensively.

At the Y.M.C.A., I came to know Randy Meyers, who was a secretary of the Washington Lions Club as it was then known. He knew of my missions to Washington and he became very much interested in what I was doing. One day he called me into his office and told me about the work and interest of the Lions clubs. He told me he could arrange for me to speak before the Washington Lions Club which met every Wednesday at noon at the Mayflower Hotel for their

usual weekly get-together. I was delighted with the suggestion, and Mr. Meyers was able to arrange for me to be the
principal speaker at their next luncheon meeting the following week.

I will never forget that wonderful and fruitful occasion.
The luncheon was well attended by the members of the club
who were some of Washington's most prominent business and
professional men. Mr. Meyers introduced me as the guest
speaker, and he told them of my many trips to Washington
on behalf of the vending stand legislation.

As my talk was to last about twenty-five minutes, I recall
it seemed like three minutes when the hands of my braille
watch told me that my time was up. I do not recall ever
having spoken to a gathering which was so attentive and so
interested in my subject. When it was all over many of the
members rushed forward to tell me how interested they were
in what I told them about the legislation. Two of these men
were Walter K. Handy, who held a prominent position with
the Potomac Electric Power Company, and William H. Dyer,
who was associated with the Perpetual Building Association.
These two men became two of my closest friends with whom
it became my pleasure and good fortune to work closely in
the years to follow.

The most outstanding event that occurred at this Lions
luncheon meeting was a private talk I had there with Randy
Meyers. He told me about the Lions International convention
which would take place in Saint Louis early that fall, and
suggested that I should be there in order to meet a certain
congressman, a Lions member, who he thought would be
interested in the vending stand idea for the blind, and perhaps take it upon himself to sponsor such a bill in the next
session of Congress. The congressman he was telling me about
was Jennings Randolph of West Virginia. Mr. Meyers promised to personally introduce me to him at the convention as
he knew the congressman planned to be there. He told me
about Congressman Randolph's active role in the Lions activi-

40

ties in West Virginia on behalf of blind persons. I made up my mind then and there to go to Saint Louis and I told Mr. Meyers I would be there.

It was in late September or early October that I drove to Saint Louis with two of my nephews to meet that member of Congress whose destiny it was to bring about the greatest vocational rehabilitation project on behalf of blind persons. Soon after my arrival in Saint Louis, I looked up Mr. Meyers who had already given the matter much thought as to where and when I would meet with Congressman Randolph. When I found him, he told me that there would be a boat ride down the Mississippi River on Wednesday night, and that the congressman would be on that boat. He would then introduce me to him.

Each day seemed like a week before that Wednesday arrived. But that Wednesday night did come, and at the opportune moment, Mr. Meyers came over to me where I was sitting with my nephews and escorted me to where Congressman Randolph was. Being the kindly and gracious person the congressman was, he made me feel as though I had known him for many years.

I recall I had plenty of time to get my story over to him. Since the subject matter consisted of employment opportunities for the adult blind, and since he was somewhat acquainted with the plight of the blind adult in West Virginia, I had quite an interested audience in the person of Congressman Randolph who, in many of his later speeches before audiences interested in the blind, would speak of this meeting with me as being my captive audience. I heard him say many times that since we were in the middle of the Mississippi River, he had no place to run.

I must have talked with him for at least an hour, or perhaps longer, as I reviewed with him my experiences with the vending stand legislation, from the reading of the article in the *Braille Mirror* to the present state of the Dunn Bill. I also told him of the opposition to the legislation that some of the workers for the blind had, so that he would understand some of the obstacles that might be in the path of legislative progress. I do not recall that I had any copies of letters, such as the one Mr. Clunk had sent me, or copies of newspaper editorials, but I told him of the kind of support I had received from various sources. Congressman Randolph at this meeting assured me he would be glad to sponsor such a bill, and I agreed to send him whatever material I had to acquaint him with the practicability of the legislation.

My next move was to acquaint Congressman Dunn with my meeting with Congressman Randolph. I remember when I approached Congressman Dunn with the matter how pleased and cooperative he was to know that another member of the House of Representatives had agreed to sponsor such legislation, and he felt that he could be of great assistance to such a colleague after the new bill was introduced.

Another very important matter had to be taken care of. A broader type of vocational rehabilitation of the adult blind had to be incorporated in the next vending stand bill. Vending stand authorization was not enough. I had obtained suggestions from various parts of the country as to how the next bill might be of assistance to blind persons in need of employment who might not fit into a vending stand project because of the lack of personality and business ability which vending stand work required. I informed Congressman Randolph of the need for this broader type of legislation, and he advised me to get the proposed legislation in proper shape and he would introduce it in the next Congress, which was the Seventy-fourth Congress.

In early December of 1934 I went to Washington where I conferred with Senator Robert J. Bulkley of Cleveland. I was always in touch with my Cleveland members of Congress with respect to the legislation, and they were always helpful in every way that they could be. I took with me my prospective vending stand bill which included some new features. It also contained a new idea with respect to the branch of the

Federal government which could best administer legislation of this kind.

The Federal agency which would administer the new vending stand legislation as outlined in my new proposal was the Vocational Rehabilitation Division of the U.S. Office of Education, which was part of the Department of the Interior. I had been persuaded to make this change by the members of the Legislative Committee of the National Rehabilitation Association, when they were in convention in Louisville in the early fall of 1934. I do not recall whether it was in September or October. That was a very busy time for me since all of my energy was directed towards getting support from all groups for the vending stand bill. I remember how greatly interested this group of men and women were in the legislation. All of them were engaged in vocational rehabilitation work, either with the Federal government or with the governments of the states from which they had come. Most of them were in direct charge of their state vocational rehabilitation programs. They pointed out to me how the Federal-state vocational rehabilitation program worked in the training and placement of physically handicapped persons. They explained to me that their experience on behalf of the blind was very limited since they left this phase of rehabilitation to the various state commissions for the blind which were set up especially to deal with the employment and welfare problems of the blind of their respective states. They pointed out, however, that if the legislation I was advocating on behalf of the blind were to be administered by their Federal bureau, cooperative arrangements with state commissions for the blind and other state agencies interested in the welfare of the blind could be worked out. I was convinced that this was the correct thing to do, and I told them that I would make the change in the new legislation.

When I arrived at Senator Bulkley's office with the new proposed vending stand bill for the blind, it was read by the senator's administrative assistant, who realized it had to be worked on and put into proper shape before Congressman Randolph could introduce it. The cooperation and interest in this legislation by Senator Bulkley's office was so great that it did not matter to them whether the legislation was being prepared for House or Senate introduction. This office directed me to one of the Senate legislative counselors whose job it would be to write the entire proposal.

I recall that the name of the person who undertook to rewrite this bill for me was a Mr. Elliott. I would meet with him for two hours every morning, and in about ten days he had completed the task. I do not know how he went about it, but it was so beautifully done, I remember I was congratulated by many of my friends around the country whose agencies for the blind were cooperating, and who saw in the new bill the opportunity to change the entire approach to the rehabilitation of blind persons if this bill became a law.

I gave the finished document to Congressman Randolph before I left Washington, and he made whatever change he had to make. Soon after the Seventy-fourth Congress convened, in January 1935, he introduced the new bill. It became known as H.R. 4688.

Soon after the introduction of the new vending stand bill, I thought it would be helpful if I could visit with Mrs. Roosevelt at the White House to explain to her the provisions of the bill and to obtain her sympathetic cooperation in getting it through Congress. I recall my appointment with her was on a Saturday afternoon late in January of 1935 and the time was set at three o'clock. I was there a bit early and the time of the appointment came and went. Ten minutes after the appointed time Mrs. Roosevelt rushed in, attired, as I was told, in riding gear. She apologized for having been late. I felt that she need not apologize to me for, after all, I had come to obtain her cooperation. But the fact that she did apologize for being late impressed me very much.

After I had explained to her the need for the legislation and what it might accomplish for the blind, she expressed an interest in it and stated she would pass the recommendation along to her husband. She had knowledge of the fact that certain other national governments had gone so far as to give their blind monopolies in certain trades. She also pointed out that the blind could certainly do many things in factories if only given a chance. I came away much encouraged.

Congressman Randolph needed someone to sponsor a companion bill in the Senate. By this time some of my American Federation of Labor friends had been in touch with him concerning the bill and it was on one of these occasions that he discussed the need for a companion bill in the Senate. One of the labor representatives suggested Senator Morris Sheppard of Texas as he had always been interested in social legislation and in labor matters. It was then that he was approached by these representatives of labor to introduce the companion bill, which he did and which became known as Senate Bill 2196.

The broader features of the Randolph-Sheppard Bill, as it was now referred to, are best described in Section I of the bill which states:

(1) Make surveys of concession stand opportunities for blind persons in Federal and other buildings in the United States;

(2) Make surveys throughout the United States of industries with a view to obtaining information that will assist blind persons to obtain employment;

(3) Make available to the public, and especially to persons and organizations engaged in work for the blind, all information obtained as a result of such surveys;

(4) Issue licenses to blind persons who are citizens of the United States twenty-one years of age or over for the operation of vending stands in Federal buildings for the vending of newspapers, periodicals, candies, tobacco products, and such other articles as may be approved for each building by the custodian thereof and by the Commissioner;

(5) Take such other steps as may be necessary and proper to carry out the provisions of this Act.

Congressman Randolph did not lose any time in contacting his fellow congressmen and obtaining from them the necessary cooperation in bringing about an early public hearing on the bill. On March 12, 1935, the congressional hearings took place before the subcommittee of the Committee on Labor.

In the consideration of the Randolph-Sheppard Bill, especially by the members making up the Committee on Labor, it is important to emphasize the role played by labor organizations in the passage of this legislation. Congressman Randolph, during his testimony before the Labor subcommittee, asked permission to include a letter which he had received from Arthur J. Lovell, vice-president and national legislative representative of the Brotherhood of Locomotive Firemen and Enginemen, which read as follows:

> Confirming our conversation of this morning with reference to the bill introduced by you in the present session of Congress in behalf of the blind, this is to advise that at meeting of December 29, 1934, held in Washington, D. C., the Railway Labor Executives Association, composed of the chief executives of the 21 standard railway labor organizations, gave consideration to the question of Federal legislation in an effort to aid the employable blind.
>
> Mr. Leonard A. Robinson is executive chairman of the Citizens Welfare Sightless Committee and has been engaged in preparation of proposed legislation on this issue.
>
> The Railway Labor Executives Association endorsed the principle of increasing employment opportunities for the blind and authorized Messrs. J. A. Farquharson, Brotherhood of Railroad Trainmen; W. D. Johnson, Order of Railway Conductors; John T. Corbett, Brotherhood of Locomotive Engineers; and the undersigned, national legislative representatives of our respective organizations, to respond accordingly, and while I am not authorized to speak for my associate national legislative representatives, I wish to assure you that I will be glad to render such assistance as may be consistently possible in support of your bill.

The hearing on the Randolph-Sheppard Bill was resumed on March 16, at which time Arthur J. Lovell testified, representing the Railway Labor Executives Association. His testimony, in part, was as follows:

The chief executives that compose the railroad labor executives have had ample time and opportunity to study this matter. We have given careful consideration to it for a number of years and we think this is the culmination of efforts in that direction. We believe that it is the most righteous legislation of the sort, the most forward-looking legislation that has come to our attention. . . . I am aware that certain things have been done for the blind by foundations and other philanthropic and well-intentioned persons, but many of those things border on paternalism. These blind are not here as beggars with hats in hand asking you to donate something. They are here, as they have a right to be here, to ask as good American citizens the privilege of earning by honest and laudable work a livelihood to which they are entitled.

The American Federation of Labor representative, S. P. Meadows, also testified on behalf of H.R. 4688. The following is, in part, his testimony:

Mr. Chairman and the gentlemen of the committee, I just want to take enough of your time to say that the American Federation of Labor is in full sympathy with the intent and purposes of this bill, and appreciating the fact that there are parties present who are vitally interested by reason of the affliction under which they have to labor and are prepared to give you all the details, it is unnecessary for me to go into them in any way, as far as the bill is concerned.

I think that we who are blessed with eyesight should be willing to render every assistance that we possibly can to those of our fellow men and women who are unfortunate enough to endeavor to try to provide for themselves under the handicap of the loss of eyesight.

Wilbur J. Dixon, chairman of the Board of Governors of the Lions International, testified as follows:

While in the city I heard of this pending bill, and I am glad to report on it as an individual.

This proposed bill was brought to my attention by the local Lions Club, of which Mr. Handy is Chairman, and I at once took it to my room and read it very carefully. I think it is one of the best bills that has been presented up to this time, and therefore I concluded to remain over and speak a good word for it. . . . We feel that this is a very worthy cause, and anything that can be done to alleviate the depression or any suffering that comes to the blind is a most worthy act.

Robert B. Irwin, executive director of the American Foundation for the Blind, was on hand to testify in favor of H.R. 4688, and the following is, in part, from his testimony:

There is probably no group of handicapped people that has more difficulty in finding jobs than blind people, and it is part of the job of the American Foundation for the Blind to find new opportunities for the blind; and in our investigations we have found that the operation of small businesses, such as small stands and small stores, offer the best opportunities for blind people with some native ability to earn their own living. Probably that line of occupation offers the best opportunity for the blind.

Within a very short time, following the hearings on H.R. 4688, the House Committee on Labor unanimously reported out the bill favorably.

Chapter 7

Organized Agencies for the Blind
Reject the Legislation

When a major objective is achieved over a period of years which was fraught with obstacles as well as pleasantries along the road of its progress, those participating in its accomplishment like to forget about the unpleasant experiences which were encountered. But when writing the history and background of the Randolph-Sheppard legislation, one cannot omit telling about the difficulties, especially when those unpleasant experiences had some bearing on the final success of the undertaking.

When the House hearings on the Randolph Bill, H.R. 4688, were over, I had an opportunity to observe the kind of support the bill got and who participated in the undertaking. As already noted, the most important and strongest support came from labor organizations. I was very happy that Robert B. Irwin of the American Foundation for the Blind could attend and his testimony was constructive. But I was disappointed in that there was no representative present at the hearings from the American Association of Workers for the Blind. This organization dates back to 1895, and in 1935 there were some 250 members belonging to the association, most of them being professional workers in the field of work for the blind.

Since I was a member of the association, but since my work was entirely voluntary with no salary attached to my efforts on behalf of the legislation, I was considered outside the scope of a professional worker for the blind. However, I was recognized for my great interest on behalf of the blind, and I was always in touch with the officers of the organization as this was part of my "unprofessional" work of keeping in touch with those in the field of work for the blind who might be in a position to do something on behalf of the legislation.

The American Association of Workers for the Blind, back in those days, held its annual conventions in June, soon after the closing of the schools for the blind, so that many teachers of the blind could attend the convention. Like all professional conventions, the association always had a very constructive and interesting agenda.

In March or April of 1935, I received a communication from the chairman of the program committee of the association, requesting that I participate in the convention, which was to be held in Louisville, Kentucky. It was suggested that I speak before the Monday morning general assembly, and that my paper cover the subject of what a college graduate believes agencies for the blind should do for the blind. I accepted the assignment immediately. I looked forward to a very constructive convention insofar as the Randolph-Sheppard legislation was concerned.

I do not recall if I was a member of the resolutions committee, which was headed by William E. Allen, superintendent of the Texas School for the Blind. I presented a resolution to the committee on behalf of the Randolph-Sheppard legislation which had as its main objective the endorsement of the legislation by the association. I recall how tremendously interested Mr. Allen was in the resolution, and it received the unanimous endorsement of the resolutions committee.

On about the third day of the convention, the association considered all of the resolutions presented to the general assembly. When Mr. Allen presented mine and recommended its adoption, I could sense the opposition which it would get

50

from some of the disgruntled members who were, perhaps, more opposed to me than to the resolution. After all, although a member of the association, I was not a "professional" worker. How should I know what was practical for the blind? After all, as it was pointed out, the bill was unconstitutional. The program could not work out well in this country.

There were many who spoke in favor of the resolution. I tried to answer the opposition with the knowledge and experience I had already gained by that time, but the turmoil was unbelievable.

Finally, one of the members, a New York City attorney, arose and moved that the resolution be tabled. The chairman of the session had no choice. That motion had to be disposed of first, according to the *Roberts Rules of Order.* If that motion carried, then the original Randolph-Sheppard resolution was dead. And so it was that the motion to table carried by a small majority, and the American Association of Workers for the Blind did not go on record in favor of the Randolph-Sheppard legislation.*

The importance of the action taken by the association, so far as I was concerned, was that it meant I would have to work harder for its passage. I was alerted to this necessity by someone who called out to me as I was leaving the room at the end of the session. He was seated near the aisle when he heard me approach as I was talking to my companion. This person was the head of a large commission for the blind. He got my attention and in no uncertain language told me he would fight me every step of the way. My only reply, as I recall, was that I would fight even harder.

About four months later, I was reminded of this individual. I was then spending most of my time in Washington,

*The American Association of Workers for the Blind today is a very thriving and useful organization under the leadership of its executive director, John L. Naler. Its present individual membership today comprises some 3,200 members. The association has grown in size commensurate with the growth and importance of work for the blind since the passage of the Randolph-Sheppard Act in 1936.

having left all of my legal work in the hands of Theodore T. Sindell with whom I was graduated at the Western Reserve University Law School. On this occasion, I was sitting in my Y.M.C.A. room and Congressman Randolph called me. He told me that a certain congressman had received a letter from one of his constituents concerning the legislation. Congressman Randolph had arranged an appointment for me to see this congressman and he wanted me to come over immediately and talk with him.

I remember it was around 11:40 A.M. The congressman received me graciously and expressed his appreciation for my coming. He told me he had received a letter from one of his constituents concerning the Randolph Bill and he needed some information from me to clear up certain objections, if I could do so. The letter came from that individual who promised me a fight to the finish. The congressman read me the two-page letter. Since this was a very important member of the House of Representatives, I realized I would have to do my level best to convince him that all the objections to the legislation contained in the letter were based on misunderstanding of the facts. I had the Clunk letter to back me up. The next fifteen minutes passed very quickly for the twelve o'clock buzzer had sounded, calling all the members of Congress to their respective chambers. I do remember most vividly how this congressman interrupted me and told me he had to attend the congressional session, thanked me for coming, and as a last gesture offered me the letter he had received. I told him I would have no need for it, and thanked him for his courtesy and understanding. I realized then that he was with me all the way, and he never once voiced any objection to the legislation or caused any delay in its consideration. I reported to Congressman Randolph when I had the opportunity to do so, and he was very pleased with the outcome of my meeting. He felt, too, I had scored a major victory.

This chapter, I feel, would not be complete without the

full text of my talk before the association, which follows in its entirety:

A College Graduate's Viewpoint as to What Organizations for the Blind Should Do for Those Without Sight

Leonard A. Robinson,
Executive Director, Citizens Welfare Sightless Committee

I think the term "college graduate" should be defined before this paper proceeds further. The fact that one might possess one or more college degrees does not in itself qualify such a person to express an opinion on what agencies for the blind should do for the blind. My undergraduate work at college, which consisted largely of the social sciences, did give me a better understanding of social problems than I would have had had I not gone to college. But even these college courses give one only a theoretical knowledge of certain situations dealing with social problems. Practical knowledge is by far the most important guide, and since my graduation from college I have acquired that practical knowledge. The school of experience is by far the best school, but the tuition is very high.

My practical knowledge of what agencies for the blind are and what they should do for the blind has been acquired during the past five years due to my active interest in the field of federal employment legislation for the blind. This work has brought me into contact with many agencies and with many workers for the blind. I have traveled over 25,000 miles on this work and at my own expense, except in a very few instances. I have attended conferences at which were present some of the country's leading workers for the blind. I have visited with certain workers at their own offices and homes, and have corresponded with scores of them, many of whom I have met only within the past few months. I have discussed the problems of self-support for the blind with all of them. Our discussions also covered many other phases of work for the blind.

I am not a professional worker for the blind, as you know, but my interest in the rehabilitation of the employable blind of this country and in the blind, generally speaking, is due to the fact that I am without sight myself. My own personal problems are not as complex as are those of the average blind person, but my perspective of the blind man's problems is far greater than that of any sighted worker for the blind, regardless of how long he might have been engaged in the work. I am a graduate of the Pennsylvania Institution for the Instruction of the Blind where I obtained a very good idea of what a person without sight can do if only given a chance. I worked my way through college selling life insurance. I am now practicing law in competition with my fellow sighted attorneys. That is my background.

The first thing, in my opinion, which the agencies for the blind can do for the blind is to forget their petty jealousies of each other and learn to cooperate with one another more harmoniously to the best interests of the blind. One worker for the blind told me not long ago that when he first came to his post after his appointment he found that the work for the blind in his state was in a very bad situation. After making a careful study of the entire situation and of his own work that he was to do, he carefully formulated a plan in which all the workers for the blind of his state were to take part. He had been greatly commended for cleaning up a bad situation in his own immediate field of work. And after cleaning his own house, so to speak, he called a conference of all the workers for the blind of his state and there presented his plan of work which would greatly assist all of them and bring very great benefits to the blind of their own respective communities. All the workers there and then agreed that his plan was perfect. They pledged their cooperation and all of them were to do certain things when they returned to their own posts. Well, instead of doing what they pledged to do, they did just the opposite. I have discussed this matter of petty jealousies and non-cooperation among workers for the blind with many of the most outstanding workers for the blind of this country, and all of them admitted that these drawbacks were quite serious and that they hindered progress in the work.

Workers for the blind should not forget that they are the indirect benefactors of the blind. In too many instances the blind are their benefactors. This is being frank and honest about the matter. I have met some workers for the blind who, because they have been engaged in the field of work for the blind for many years, are of the opinion that no one, without previous experience in the field, knows anything about the blind and because of this lack of experience such a person cannot express an opinion or make a constructive suggestion in the field of work for the blind. Such a person, in their opinion, could not be called upon to do anything constructive for the blind. I have also met some

54

workers who refused to cooperate with anyone unless they were called upon at the very beginning to have a hand in the work. In these instances I have found these professional workers refusing to cooperate because of selfish reasons, fearing that they might be taken from the limelight either temporarily or permanently.

I once met a person who had only been in the field of work for the blind about six months, but during that time had done a splendid job for the undertaking was a very big one. Three months later I met another worker for the blind in quite a different part of the country and happened to mention my having met this other worker. Upon the mention of this worker's name, the person to whom I was speaking became somewhat snobbish and remarked that my acquaintance had had no previous experience in the field of work for the blind. It so happens that this "inexperienced worker" is now present at this A.A.W.B. convention with a record of accomplishments which any worker for the blind of many years experience could envy.

The second thing which agencies for the blind can do for the blind is to bring to the attention of their respective communities the abilities of the blind and what the blind can do if only given a chance. This can best be done by educational weeks for the blind held each year, and the benefits which result from such educational weeks should be followed up during the remaining fifty-one weeks of the year. There is pending in Congress now a bill introduced in the Senate by Senator Bailey providing for a national educational week for the blind to be held the first week in May. The purpose of the bill is "to stimulate nation-wide interest in the blind citizens of the United States and its possessions; to demonstrate to the general public the various occupations of the blind; to show how the blind citizens of the United States and its possessions may become self-supporting and, in a measure, lessen the burden already imposed upon the taxpayers of the nation; to demonstrate the best methods of conserving eyesight and preventing blindness; and to make public every method which may be used to improve the condition of the blind generally."

Every conscientious worker for the blind should get in back of this bill and work for its passage. And when this bill becomes a law and when these educational weeks become a reality, every effort should be made on the part of every worker for the blind to bring to the attention of the sighted that persons without sight are normal, human beings just as in the case of the sighted. Dr. O. H. Burritt of the school for the blind which I attended always did contend that the blind are just as normal as are the sighted. If the blind have inferiority complexes, that is because their training either at school or at home has been bad, or because society has not given them a fair chance in life. When they are refused employment by employers who wonder what they can do, being without sight, they naturally begin to feel that perhaps they are inferior. When their own members of their family are somewhat ashamed of them because they cannot see, that, too, causes them to feel inferior, and this condition should be remedied by the field workers wherever it is possible to do so. One sighted worker for the blind who has been in the work for more than twenty-five years told me that the blind were a bunch of dumb persons. I wonder if this worker tells everyone that! If so, then how can that worker expect to find work for the blind in that worker's respective community? It so happens that I know what the situation is in that worker's community with respect to the blind being employed, and the blind, for the most part, are on relief rolls.

The third thing which agencies for the blind can do for the blind is to cooperate harmoniously in the furtherance of the Randolph-Sheppard Blind Employment Bill, H.R. 4688-S. 2196 now before Congress. This bill, if enacted into law, would permit worthy blind persons to operate news, candy, and tobacco stands in federal buildings. It would authorize a national survey to be made of non-federal buildings wherein similar concession stand opportunities might be obtained. It is apparent that not all the employable blind have the necessary business ability and the personality required to operate such a small business, and so another national survey of industries is authorized to be made wherein the blind can be trained and given suitable employment. Thus, a national, uniform, and coordinate plan of rehabilitating the blind of this country will be brought into existence if this bill is enacted into law, bringing into being a rehabilitation project similar to that in Canada. Placement officers will be given special training, and this feature is one of the most important ones of the bill. Joseph F. Clunk, National Supervisor of Industrial Employment, Canadian National Institute for the Blind, whose placement work in Canada has become internationally famous, has unqualifiedly endorsed this bill. He is to speak at this convention of the importance of placement work. No new federal or state agencies will be brought about by this legislation as existing ones will administer the project in close cooperation with both private and public agencies for the blind of this country. More than twenty million persons in the United States today have endorsed this bill through their affiliated organizations and at the time of this writing, the House Labor Committee has reported the bill out favorably. If this bill does not go through it will be because the workers for the blind are non-cooperative. I am happy to state that many workers for the blind have done excellent work in furthering this legislation. They realize that if this bill goes through, they will be more able to be of service to the blind of their respective communities.

Public sentiment is in favor of this legislation as evidenced by editorial comment. The country's three largest newspaper syndicates—Hearst, Scripps-Howard, and Paul Block—have come out editorially for this legislation. I quote from one of the Hearst editorials which appeared in the Washington Times of February 19, 1935: "This bill deserves prompt and favorable consideration by both houses of Congress. It would take care of a group of our people who are in distress and who are not being reached by any of the vast rehabilitation experiments which the government is conducting. The appealing part about the measure is that its degree of success depends entirely upon the energy and ambition of those who would be benefited."

I quote from one of the Scripps-Howard editorials which appeared in the Cleveland Press of March 18, 1935: "The federal relief administrator has said that persons on relief rolls actually despise their position in asking the dole. They want work to earn their bread. The same applies to the blind. Unable to compete with the more fortunate, the sightless have had to gather the few left-over crumbs of charity during the depression. . . . No great sums are asked in the way of appropriations—merely enough to carry the actual cost. Adequate safeguards exclude unqualified persons. This can be done better by law than by executive order. . . . Congress can render a needed service to the blind by approval of the Randolph Bill, which establishes a broad plan of rehabilitation applicable to all who can qualify."

One of the Paul Block papers, the Pittsburgh Post-Gazette, even suggests that state legislatures can follow the example of Congress. The entire editorial is so good and at the same time short, I will quote it in full here. It is entitled "Practical Help for the Blind."

> Genuine as Gibraltar, and equally unshakable, is the general sympathy for persons afflicted with blindness and, while normal in other respects, cruelly handicapped in the

business of making a living. No bill in Congress could be much more free from opposition than the one providing for operation of news, cigar, and candy stands in federal buildings, by blind persons. Equally safe against attack is the further provision for small loans to start such persons in these small businesses.

So excellent is this plan of assistance by the public to its sightless members, it might well be picked up by the state legislatures and bills passed providing for similar arrangements in the state buildings. Legislators voting in favor could be quite sure of having the public with them.

There are other interesting bills in Congress affecting the welfare of the blind but time and space will not permit any mention of them here.

In the February "Outlook" for this year was an article written by Dr. Edward E. Allen, one of the world's leading workers for the blind. This was a paper which Dr. Allen had prepared entitled "The Education of Blind Children of School Age" which he presented at a conference on the education of the handicapped at New York University, March 10, 1934. I quote from Dr. Allen's paper:

It would help and encourage if some industrial occupation were their monopoly, as massage has been to the blind of Japan. There is before Congress a bill proposed to open postoffices and other federal buildings to stand-keeping by blind people. If this becomes a law, our schools should begin to train for the many new opportunities it will open up. The training which aims to increase the selling capacity must educate for personal acceptability as an essential to business success.

Dr. Allen referred to the bill with which I had a great deal to do. This present one is by far the better of the two, and has been hailed as the best of its kind ever introduced in Congress. The former one was not endorsed by our Ohio Commission for the Blind; the present one was enthusiastically and unanimously endorsed by our commission on February 6, 1935. The same is true of many, many other associations for the blind. So I take it that the spirit of cooperation is becoming stronger among the agencies and workers for the blind, and I sincerely hope that this A.A.W.B. convention will go down in history as the turning point in the field of work for the blind in this country. That turning point, I mean, is to be upward. What we must all do is to understand each other. We must learn to be open and above board and be frank and honest with our opinions. The truth never hurts if it is told in the right spirit. The trouble lies in the fact that it is never taken in the right spirit. Constructive criticism is always helpful. Do let us understand each other in the proper light so that the blind of this country might share with their sighted friends the happiness and some of the luxuries to which man is entitled.

Chapter 8

Final Steps to Passage of H.R. 4688

The Louisville convention which turned down the Randolph-Sheppard Bill was quite a disappointment to me. The big thing in my favor was that I was an optimist. Nothing could make me feel that I was working for something which had no chance of passage.

I had motored down to Louisville with my nephew in a brand new Oldsmobile. I had just worn out a 1930 Oldsmobile which the Cleveland dealer recommended I get rid of as he knew how important motor transportation was to me for my legislative lobbying work. When I took my old car in for a service check four days before I started on my Louisville trip, he called me over and told me that if I sold my car outright, he would sell me another brand new one at cost. I took him up on that at once and he sent me to a used car dealer a few blocks away. There I agreed to sell my old car for $175 and the dealer took it on a consignment basis. He would charge me ten dollars if a sale went through. Within thirty minutes after my nephew, who used to drive me, and I got home I received a call from this used car dealer who told me to bring down my bill of sale, that he had a customer who wanted my car. Within thirty minutes I was back with him. The deal went through, and I took my $165 over to my Oldsmobile dealer and he had just the car I wanted—a two-door green sedan. The list price was $893.00, but I bought it for $721.40, and with my $165 down payment, I had no trouble financing the rest of the purchase price.

So I drove with my nephew to Louisville in a new car, and after the convention was over, started out for Knoxville, Tennessee, where one of my sisters still lived with her family, and there I started a campaign for the passage of the Randolph-Sheppard Bill.

Since I was well known in Knoxville, having been born there and a graduate of the University of Tennessee, I had little difficulty in forming a committee which became known as the Knoxville Committee for the Blind. I visited the old university campus and was able to obtain the cooperation of President James D. Hoskins who became very much interested in the legislation. We planned a banquet which took place at the Andrew Johnson Hotel, at which some one hundred persons were in attendance. President Hoskins acted as banquet chairman and honorary chairman of the Executive Committee for the Blind.

President Hoskins, in his inspired message to the banquet guests, spoke of the need for legislation such as the Randolph-Sheppard Bill in order to bring self-sufficiency to thousands of blind persons who would be taken from relief rolls, but who were competent to operate a small business such as the legislation would provide. He urged everyone to write to their senators and congressmen in Washington requesting them to vote for the measure.

I recall that when I got up to speak following President Hoskins's remarks, I was so stunned by the compliments showered on me by President Hoskins that I forgot my opening remarks which I had planned in advance. I then resorted to my old style of talking by telling my audience what I believed the legislation would do for the blind if Congress passed it. I emphasized the importance of removing blind persons from welfare rolls by giving them an opportunity to earn their own livelihood. In this respect, I quoted from an essay titled "The Eight Degrees of Charity," written by the eminent Jewish philosopher, Moses Maimonides, 1135-1204:

> Lastly, the *eighth,* and the most meritorious of all, is to antici-
> pate charity by preventing poverty; namely, to assist the reduced
> fellowman, either by a considerable gift, or a sum of money, or
> by teaching him a trade, or by putting him in the way of business,
> so that he may earn an honest livelihood, and not be forced to
> the dreadful alternative of holding out his hand for charity. This
> is the highest step and the summit of charity's golden ladder.

During my stay in Knoxville, the committee was successful in organizing a workshop for the blind where blind persons could be taught manual crafts and whose products could be sold, both retail and wholesale. Miss Florence Arp of Knoxville was put in charge of the workshop which later became a thriving business.

Back in Cleveland after my Knoxville trip, I was always busy gaining support for the legislation from whatever source with which I had a contact. As I was a member of the college fraternity Phi Alpha, with chapters in many states, I was assisted by the fraternity secretary in spreading the word around to the various chapters to get as many as possible of my fraternity brothers to write to their senators and congressmen in support of the Randolph-Sheppard Bill.

In late December of 1935, the national convention of the Phi Alpha Fraternity was held in New York City. I attended this convention. At one of the afternoon sessions which I attended, I walked over to the presiding officer and asked to be excused as I had a very important appointment with Rabbi Stephen S. Wise with whom I had been in correspondence for the past two years concerning the legislation but had never met personally. The appointment was at five-thirty that afternoon which was on December 31. I was told by the presiding officer to take my seat and in a few minutes I would be excused.

In about ten minutes one of the principal officers of the fraternity took the rostrum, and in a glowing tribute to one

62

of the Phi Alpha members, he pointed out how this member was very active in bringing economic self-sufficiency to his fellow blind. By then I knew he was talking about me. I was called to the platform to accept the Phi Alpha Illustrious Alumnus Award. In my acceptance speech I made it clear that I had not done anything to merit this honor, but that I was trying to accomplish something. I told them I could not let them down and would try all the harder to get the Randolph-Sheppard Bill through so that I would merit their great tribute to me. I explained that I had this very important meeting with Rabbi Wise and excused myself from further participation in the meeting for that day.

My meeting with Rabbi Wise was one I shall never forget. He was a very busy man. I visited with him at his Free Synagogue study. Many persons had been in to see him that late afternoon from all parts of the country.

Rabbi Wise got to me around six o'clock. He was very kind and very understanding of what I was trying to do for my fellow blind. In one respect that meeting with him reminded me of my visit with President-elect Roosevelt in 1933. Both these men, very busy and much sought after, talked with me about my activities as though they had nothing else on their minds but the desire and interest in wanting to do something which would bring about some measure of good for those adult blind persons who wanted to earn their own way through life.

That evening at the fraternity dance I mentioned to the young lady with whom I was keeping company in a somewhat serious way, that I was so impressed with Rabbi Wise that I was going to keep him in mind to officiate at my wedding when that time arrived.

On March 16, 1936, I received the good news from Congressman Randolph stating: "Blind bill just passed House few minutes ago. Letter follows."

Two days later I received a clipping from a Washington friend, Harry S. Wender, which he had taken from the Washington *Herald.* The headline of this article was to the effect that, with the blind legislation which just passed the House, the blind would be taking over the government cafeterias. That frightened me, because there was never any intention that the Randolph-Sheppard Bill would eventually turn over to the blind the existing cafeterias. I arranged for my nephew to drive me to Washington the following day. I visited the office of the *Herald* but could not find out who wrote the article.

I then went to the office of John A. Kratz, chief of the Vocational Rehabilitation Division of the United States Office of Education. I had spent many long hours with Mr. Kratz as his department would be responsible for the administration of the Randolph-Sheppard legislation. I told Mr. Kratz that if the Public Buildings Administration, which Federal department had charge of all the government cafeterias, believed they would lose these cafeterias to the blind if the vending stand bill ever became law, that they would do all they could to bring pressure upon the Senate to defeat the recently House-passed legislation. He agreed with me and advised me to make an appointment with the general counsel of the Public Buildings Administration, Louis Frick, and to explain to him that the cafeterias would never be transferred over to the blind.

I met with Mr. Frick the following day. He was quite aware of my activities on behalf of the legislation. He received me courteously and with a great deal of interest in what I had to tell him.

I do not recall any meeting I ever had with anyone concerning the legislation where I put more effort in my arguments to sell the cause and the importance of the legislation to the blind. I realized that he was my last barrier. I think I spent about an hour with him. I must have convinced him of my sincerity, as he admitted to me that it was he who wrote the letter bearing the name of Secretary of the Interior Harold L. Ickes, which letter was sent to the two committees of the House and Senate handling the Randolph-Sheppard Bill and which letter in no uncertain terms recommended that the legislation should be defeated. This admission by Mr. Frick was just another way of telling me that he now understood the need of the legislation for the blind and that he would not be a stumbling block in its passage.

In his letter dated April 24, 1936, which was sent to Senator David I. Walsh, chairman of the Committee on Education and Labor, Mr. Ickes wrote the following:

> ... the bill is objectionable in that it excludes from the operation of stands able-bodied persons and persons incapacitated by reasons other than blindness. There are a number of vending stands located in buildings under the jurisdiction of this Department where the employment of able-bodied persons is necessary because blind persons cannot meet the requirements. I feel that unemployed able-bodied persons who can perform more effective service than blind persons in certain cases deserve consideration, since they cannot command the same public assistance and sympathy as the blind.

From the above it is quite clear that Mr. Frick also thought the blind would take over the ten or twelve vending stands that the government cafeterias were in charge of in some Federal buildings. I made it clear to Mr. Frick that we had no intention of taking over either the cafeterias or these stands which were then in existence and being run by sighted able-bodied persons.

When I had finished with the Public Buildings Administration, I made up my mind that I would remain on in Washington to take care of any other important items which might come up. As the House had passed the bill without dissent, its next course of action was before the Senate. I worked closely with Senator Sheppard who advised me that the Senate would take up the House bill instead of going through separate hearings on the Senate companion bill, S. 2196. He told me that there was opposition to a portion of the bill from the Bureau of the Budget, and suggested I meet with the acting director of the budget, Daniel W. Bell, as soon as possible. His office obtained an appointment for me.

When I reached Mr. Bell's office, I was able to meet with him personally instead of with his administrative secretary. He was in favor of the legislation, but he pointed out that his opposition was based on the provision in Section 3 which provided, in part, "The Office of Education is authorized to purchase stand equipment out of funds hereinafter authorized to be appropriated, and, subject to such rules and regulations as he may prescribe, to lend such stand equipment to the various State commissions for the blind. . . ." Mr. Bell contended that the various state boards of vocational education which were responsible for the state vocational rehabilitation programs had the money with which to purchase this equipment.

I explained to Mr. Bell just how these state rehabilitation programs operated, and that I was familiar with their lack of funds for this equipment. I pointed out to him that the various programs of rehabilitation did very little for blind persons as they referred all such cases to the commissions for the blind in those states where there were such commissions, and in those states where there were no such commissions, private agencies for the blind were designated to handle the problems of blind persons to the extent possible. I further pointed out to him that the vending stand equipment would have to be especially designed for each Federal building location, and that such equipment would be somewhat costly. He was not impressed, and his final advice was to strike the equipment section from the bill.

A week later I was called into Senator Sheppard's office for a conference with the senator. He told me that Senator David I. Walsh, whose committee in the Senate was handling the legislation, advised him to delete the reference to the vending stand equipment, and we would have no trouble from then on. I recall the advice he gave me. He said, "Leonard, let us delete this section. Half a loaf is better than no

66

loaf at all. Let us get the bill passed and in a year come back and we will see what can be done."

Section 3 was deleted along with other very minor changes, and in the early days of June, the Senate passed H.R. 4688 with amendments. I was then in very close contact with Congressman Randolph, and since we both agreed that what the Senate passed was the best we could hope for, we decided that a joint conference committee was not necessary. It is before such a committee that House and Senate differences are thrashed out. The Senate version came before the House which accepted the Senate amendments and that was the final step.

I was sitting in the House gallery when this took place. I recall that when the House took its final step, Congressman William P. Connery, Jr., chairman of the House Labor Committee, arose and congratulated Congressman Randolph on getting through such an important and meritorious piece of legislation.

Following this action, Congressman Randolph motioned to my companion to come down. When we met Congressman Randolph on the lower level, he took us out to the top of the Capitol steps where he had a photographer waiting for us. That was the most important photograph I was ever in, and none since then can compare with it in importance.

A few days before the House action took place, I made my rounds of the offices of the two Cleveland congressmen who had been so helpful to me during this long struggle for the legislation. My purpose in seeing them was to tell them what was going to take place and to be prepared for it. One of these congressmen was Congressman Robert Crosser. When I told him that the end was near at hand, he said to me, "Leonard, aren't you asking us to bring about something that the blind cannot do? How can a blind man tell the difference between a quarter, a dime, and a half-dollar?" I was really taken aback at this question and at his attitude. I told him that the blind had a sensitive touch, and that he could test

Congressman Jennings Randolph, left, and Leonard A. Robinson. Picture taken at top of Capitol steps following final passage of Randolph-Sheppard Bill.

me. He did and I had no trouble at all. I recall telling him to drop any coin he wanted to and by the sound alone I could tell him what it was. He did, and I had no trouble at all. He then assured me that he was quite convinced that we were working on a very practical project and promised to do everything he could to see the bill through.

I have always contended that the greatest support for the legislation came from organized labor. I have already referred to the testimony before the House Labor subcommittee of S. P. Meadows of the American Federation of Labor and that of Arthur J. Lovell, who represented the railroad brotherhoods. I felt extremely happy when I received the two letters which follow:

AMERICAN FEDERATION OF LABOR

Executive Council
President, WILLIAM GREEN.
Secretary-Treasurer, FRANK MORRISON
A. F. of L. Building, Washington, D. C.

First Vice-President, FRANK DUFFY,
Carpenters' Building, Indianapolis, Ind.
Second Vice-President, T. A. RICKERT,
621 Bible House, New York, N. Y.
Third Vice-President, MATTHEW WOLL,
570 Lexington Ave., New York, N. Y.
Fourth Vice-President, JOHN COEFIELD,
Machinists' Building, Washington, D. C.
Fifth Vice-President, ARTHUR O. WHARTON,
Machinists' Building, Washington, D. C.
Sixth Vice-President, JOSEPH N. WEBER,
1450 Broadway, New York, N. Y.
Seventh Vice-President, G. M. BUGNIAZET,
1200 Fifteenth St., N. W., Washington, D. C.

Eighth Vice-President, GEO. M. HARRISON
Railway Clerks' Bldg., Cincinnati, O.
Ninth Vice-President, DANIEL J. TOBIN,
222 East Michigan Street, Indianapolis, Ind.
Tenth Vice-President, WILLIAM L. HUTCHESON,
Carpenters' Building, Indianapolis, Ind.
Eleventh Vice-President, DAVID DUBINSKY,
3 West Sixteenth Street, New York, N. Y.
Twelfth Vice-President, HARRY C. BATES,
815 Fifteenth St., N.W., Washington, D. C.
Thirteenth Vice-President, EDWARD J. GAINOR,
408 A. F. of L. Building, Washington, D. C.
Fourteenth Vice-President, W. D. MAHON,
260 Vernor Highway, East, Detroit, Mich.
Fifteenth Vice-President, FELIX H. KNIGHT,
400-403 Carmen's Bldg., Kansas City, Mo.

LONG DISTANCE TELEPHONE NATIONAL 3870-1-2-3-4
CABLE ADDRESS, AFEL.

Washington, D. C.

July 8, 1936.

Mr. Leonard A. Robinson, Chairman,
Citizens Welfare Sightless Committee,
1508 Standard Building,
Cleveland, Ohio.

Dear Mr. Robsinson:

  The legislation secured in the interest of
the blind in the last Congress, to which you refer in
your letter of June 29, will be of incalculable benefit.

  I wish to congratulate you for the persis-
tency with which you sought the legislation.

       Very truly yours,

       President,
       American Federation of Labor.

-EGT

AMERICAN FEDERATION OF LABOR

Washington, D. C.

July 8, 1936.

Mr. Leonard A. Robinson, Chairman,
Citizens Welfare Sightless Committee,
1508 Standard Building,
Cleveland, Ohio.

Dear Mr. Robinson:

     Everybody interested in the bills you had introduced in Congress believe you deserve the hearty congratulations of those for whom you acted.

     Undoubtedly, as you say, Labor was very helpful. Your reference to the aid given by the Legislative Committee of the American Federation of Labor is appreciated.

Very truly yours,

W. C. Roberts

Chairman,
Legislative Committee,
American Federation of Labor.

-EGT

70

On June 20, 1936, President Franklin D. Roosevelt signed the bill into law, thus closing a chapter in history benefiting the adult blind of the United States, which was destined to become the most practical and helpful piece of legislation ever enacted into law on behalf of the sightless.

Of the many scores of newspapers around the country which endorsed the Randolph-Sheppard Bill, the newspaper which stood out in my mind more than any other was the Cleveland *News*. It was this newspaper which first recognized the importance of such legislation. Its editor, Earl Martin, always saw to it that the movement got full coverage in his newspaper. When I wrote to him from Washington informing him of the action President Roosevelt took on June 20, he must have been just as elated as I. The following editorial in the Cleveland *News* appeared July 2, 1936. Since the newspaper is no longer in existence, I take the liberty to present the editorial in full:

Mr. Robinson's Gallant Fight

We don't know when we've been more thrilled and more humble before the story of a man's single-handed fight against almost overwhelming odds.

But we are that before the story of Leonard A. Robinson, who today has won his five-year fight to help the blind help themselves. His story is a story of high courage and stanch devotion to an ideal. At seven an accident destroyed his left eye, and by the time he was 14 his right eye had become affected and he was permanently blind. And at 14, when a boy is in a curiously sensitive, adolescent state, such a blow is altogether crushing.

But undeterred, he attended a school for the blind, then the University of Tennessee, until by the drudge of daily labor which only the blind student can know, he was able to be graduated from Western Reserve university in 1929 as a full-fledged lawyer.

Then forgetting himself (who had no need of such aid) he set out single-handed to persuade the government to permit blind men and women to operate news and candy stands in federal buildings. He drew up the law himself. He organized a local Citizens' Welfare Sightless committee to raise $3,000 for expenses.

71

From Cleveland to Washington and back again he tirelessly journeyed, seeking support.

Reporters of the News to whom he talked will not forget his visits. Led by a boy, he came into the editorial rooms, his sightless eyes hidden by dark glasses, to stand by the reporter's desk and explain his mission. Everything that was to be thought of, he thought of. Everything that was to be done, he did. They have rarely seen such a glowing determination, such a constant crusade on the behalf of others.

Finally, after he had drawn up his bill twice; after it had become the Randolph-Sheppard bill; after it had languished in committee; after he had buttonholed congressmen, written letters, engaged in painstaking journey after journey again—finally, it was passed by the House three months ago, then by the Senate.

And now it has been signed by President Roosevelt, and becomes law. Mr. Robinson has done a noble thing, one for which the sightless of the country will thank him for years to come.

We know of no better use to which we could put this editorial space today than to use it to thus' pay tribute to him and his achievement.

The five years I spent promoting the vending stand legislation through Congress were filled with many interesting and thrilling experiences. Meeting with so many interesting persons in many walks of life was an education in itself.

While in Washington and awaiting President Roosevelt's signing of the Randolph-Sheppard Bill, I met the most important person of all. She was Miss Sonia Berman who had just arrived from her home in Philadelphia to work for the Veterans Administration. Seven months later we were married, and Rabbi Stephen S. Wise officiated at the wedding. We have one son, Louis, who is a graduate of Miami University of Ohio in architecture and city planning.

Chapter 9

Federal Implementation
of the Randolph-Sheppard Act

In September 1936, John W. Studebaker, who was the commissioner of the United States Office of Education, called a conference of workers for the blind which took place in Washington for the purpose of working out administrative procedures for the Randolph-Sheppard Act. There were about forty persons who attended this conference. John A. Kratz of the Vocational Rehabilitation Division, an agency within the Office of Education, explained that the law would be put into effect as soon as the administrative procedures could be set up.

In October, "Suggested Principles and Procedures" were issued, covering such subjects as selection of buildings in which to place stands, location of stands in buildings, stand equipment, ownership of concession, equipment and stock, articles to be vended, selection of operator, training of operator and supervision of operation of stands. This last subject was somewhat controversial when the legislation was passed, requiring a good deal of diplomacy for years to come, since the independent spirit of stand operators was involved.

The legal definition of blindness, as stated in the Randolph-Sheppard Act in Section 7, was as follows:

> The term "blind person" means a person (1) having not more than 10 per centum visual acuity in the better eye with correc-

tion, or (2) whose vision is so impaired that regular employment cannot be obtained due to this infirmity.

The administration of the act finally got under way in July 1937 when Joseph F. Clunk was persuaded to leave his very fine and responsible position with the Canadian National Institute for the Blind in Toronto, Canada, and come to Washington to head up the Randolph-Sheppard services in the U.S. Office of Education of the Department of the Interior. We were very fortunate that Mr. Clunk could do so, and he lost no time in getting started.

The legislation provided that the licensing agency in each state should be a state functioning agency. Since the Randolph-Sheppard Act included other provisions for the rehabilitation of blind persons in addition to the vending stand program, such licensing agencies within the various states would take on added responsibilities which included the placement of blind persons in industries.

Section 1 of the act provided as follows:

(1) Make surveys of concession stand opportunities for blind persons in Federal and other buildings in the United States;
(2) Make surveys throughout the United States of industries with a view to obtaining information that will assist blind persons to obtain employment;
(3) Make available to the public, and especially to persons and organizations engaged in work for the blind, all information obtained as a result of such surveys.

As soon as Mr. Clunk could obtain an adequate staff of trained personnel, one of the major activities of his department, Services for the Blind, included specialized training of personnel engaged by the state agencies in the placement of blind persons. Courses were also held for thirty-seven state workers engaged in placing blind persons in business enterprise programs. One course was conducted for eleven persons engaged in placing blind persons in agricultural activities.

As everyone in work for the blind was familiar with the successful work carried on by Mr. Clunk in Canada, it was not too difficult for him to carry out his basic philosophy with respect to the vending stand program.

One of Mr. Clunk's great assets was his belief in the abilities of blind persons. He knew that they could be successful in many undertakings, and he also knew that they could fail in whatever they pursued if proper training was not provided for them prior to their various pursuits. In the vending stand program he realized that care should be taken in the selection of the operator. Equal in importance was the kind of vending stand equipment and accessories for each location. In practically all cases, such equipment had to be made to order. The finest woods and materials were recommended. To attract business, the vending stand location had to be attractive. The merchandise had to be displayed attractively. Each location was to be kept clean, and an adequate stock of merchandise was to be on hand at all times. The customer was not going to go out of his way to make a purchase at one of these stands just because the operator was blind. He had to be an up-to-date businessman conducting his business in a business-like way.

On April 1, 1938, I was appointed to the vending stand administration as assistant to the supervisor. Mr. Clunk was supervisor.

One of my first duties was to organize the vending stand program in the District of Columbia. / side 4

The Randolph-Sheppard Act and its ensuing rules and regulations recognized the state commissions for the blind, where there were such commissions, to be the licensing state agency to administer the vending stand program as authorized by the act. These commissions were engaged in the rehabilitation of blind persons such as existed at that time. In those states where there were no such commissions for the blind, the vending stand licensing authority was assigned to other state agencies for the blind wherever the state laws authorized these special units to provide such services. In other states the phase of vocational rehabilitation and the vending stand licensing authority were included in the work of these general rehabilitation agencies, which were units of the state boards of education.

The Randolph-Sheppard Act, for the purpose of the vending stand program, regarded the District of Columbia as any other state. The only public agency in the District at the time engaged in vocational rehabilitation for the adult population was the Vocational Rehabilitation Service under the direction of H. C. Corpening. This agency, in fact, was a field office of the United States Office of Education which Federal department administered the work of the Vocational Rehabilitation Division. In 1954, under the amendments to the Vocational Rehabilitation Act, this District program became a part of the District of Columbia government under the supervision of the Board of Commissioners of the District Government.

One of the first acts of Mr. Clunk's administration was to license the Vocational Rehabilitation Service of the District with its responsibility for the vending stand program.

In 1937 there were between seventy and eighty Federal buildings located in the District of Columbia, and in almost every one of them there was need for a vending stand to be operated by a blind person. To take advantage of this situation seemed to pose an insurmountable problem. There was no provision in the Randolph-Sheppard Act for the purchase of vending stand equipment. That provision of the act had to be deleted.

In order to get the vending stand program in the District started, Mr. Clunk borrowed from his experience in Canada, which provided for an overall six percent of their total merchandise sales to be paid by the vending stand operators. For this payment, the vending stand operator would receive his vending stand equipment and accessories, together with an initial stock of merchandise. He would also receive whatever supervisory assistance he would require with day-to-day services to the extent necessary to make his vending stand operation produce the maximum return possible. The vending stand operator would not be considered an employee but rather a self-employed person. He would be entitled to all of the net profits of the stand, and these profits would reflect his business ability, initiative, and good management.

Since Mr. Corpening's government office could not borrow any money with which to purchase vending stand equipment and stocks of merchandise for the stands, and since it could not handle money for the day-to-day operations, an arrangement was worked out with the Welfare and Recreation Association, as it was then known, which association managed the cafeterias in the Federal buildings. This association, which was quasi-public in its operations, was controlled by the Public Buildings Administration of the Department of Interior. The association agreed to provide the necessary vending stand equipment and initial stocks of merchandise, be responsible for the day-to-day supervision, collect all moneys and pay to each operator each month the net proceeds his stand earned. For this service the association retained the six percent of the sales which the vending stands experienced during the month. Out of this six percent the association would reimburse itself for the cost of the vending stand equipment, initial stocks of merchandise, and for anything else the vending stand locations required. Any amount which remained over and above these reimbursements, including personal services, went into the general treasury of the association. Under this plan, the first vending stand under the Randolph-Sheppard Act in the District went into operation in early January of 1938.

When I came into the program in April 1938, there were four vending stands in operation under this arrangement. One of my first duties was to improve the program and make it more practical. At that time there was one private agency catering to the needs, in a very limited way, of the blind of the District of Columbia. It was then known as the Columbia Polytechnic Institute for the Blind. Its major activity was chair caning which blind persons could do very well, but there were only some five or six blind persons engaged in that work. They were situated in a six-room brick house which was then located at 1808 H Street, N.W. A meeting with their director was arranged for the purpose of ascertaining whether they would assume the obligations and duties of the vending stand program in the District of Columbia together with the Vocational Rehabilitation Service. It was quite obvious at the time that the stand program was self-sufficient with money to spare for other vocational rehabilitation projects for blind persons. They refused to accept our proposal. This was, no doubt, based upon their bad experience with an attempt to operate a vending stand program in 1935, together with the Vocational Rehabilitation Service, pending the passage of the Randolph-Sheppard Act. Some seventeen stands were installed in various Federal buildings in the District, and their installation and operation were so badly handled, that by the time Mr. Clunk came upon the scene in July of 1937, there were only six left and these were threatened with closure. In fact, these stands should never have been approved in the first place as there was no one in authority who had the know-how or the experience of running such a program. There is no doubt but what they prejudiced the various government departments who had to approve or disapprove the Randolph-Sheppard Bill before Congress. Mr. Clunk was able to keep these last six stands in existence until they could be taken over officially by the District program. They were given whatever assistance they needed of a temporary nature, and because of this, they were allowed to remain in existence and the blind operators were at least kept on the job.

At this point I borrowed from my experience of the past and approached the members of the Washington Lions Club with whom I had kept in close contact since I first met them in 1934. The objective was to bring about a new nonprofit organization for the blind and incorporate it under the laws that applied in the District of Columbia. The several Lions club members we talked to were very much interested in the proposal. As many of them as would be needed were willing

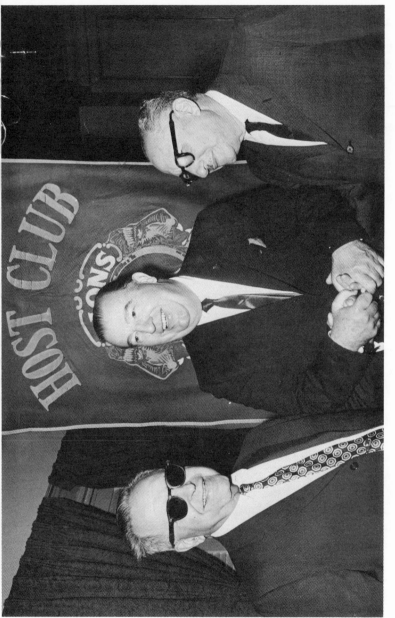

Senator Jennings Randolph congratulating Leonard Robinson, right, and Joseph Clunk, left, on the occasion of the thirtieth anniversary of the Randolph-Sheppard Act, June 1966, at the Washington Host Lions Club.

to serve as officers and members of the board of directors. They understood how the program could be self-supporting, and that aspect of it they appreciated. They agreed to assume all the responsibilities such a program would entail, and without compensation for their time spent, they were eager to get under way at the earliest date possible.

In the latter part of 1938 we organized the Washington Society for the Blind. Walter K. Handy of the Potomac Electric Power Company became president. William H. Dyer of the Perpetual Building Association became vice-president. Archibald McLachlen of the McLachlen Banking Corporation acted as treasurer. Mrs. Ross T. McIntire, wife of Admiral McIntire—President Roosevelt's private physician—became secretary. I had known the McIntires for five years, and had spent many pleasant hours with them at their beautiful home in Spring Valley. I had interested them in the Randolph-Sheppard legislation, and they were of assistance to me in making important contacts. They had been impressed with my meeting with President-elect Roosevelt in January 1933. When the President's Committee on Employment of the Handicapped was brought about in 1946, Dr. McIntire became its first chairman. He had become interested in the problems of the physically handicapped as a result of his interest in the vending stand program. Charles A. Peters, who directed the activities of the Public Buildings Administration, agreed to serve on the board of directors. His government department had the last say in whether a vending stand would be permitted to be installed in a Federal building almost anywhere in the United States, as his department was in charge of the maintenance of the vast majority of such buildings. Other prominent government and business men also served on the board.

One of the first things that had to be accomplished was the takeover from the Welfare and Recreation Association. The society would have to borrow money with which to pay the association for any unpaid balance due for original equipment and stocks of merchandise.

Since the Washington Society for the Blind was a non-profit organization, arrangements were made with two vending machine companies to make installations of vending machines in government buildings where there were no cafeterias or snack bars and in other non-Federal buildings, and the commissions from such placements would be paid to the Washington Society for the Blind. Before many months went by, the income from these placements was two hundred dollars a month. I sought, in the meantime, the assistance of the Reconstruction Finance Corporation, which government department would guarantee loans to businesses in need of financial help and which were not obtainable in any other way. At first they were not interested, but after their representative looked into the matter and realized that the Washington Society for the Blind was engaged in a self-supporting project, plus the fact that it was receiving other income from vending machine installations, the Reconstruction Finance Corporation finally guaranteed the fifteen-thousand-dollar loan which the society obtained from the McLachlen Banking Corporation, and which was guaranteed to the extent of 75 percent. The loan was for five years, but it turned out that it was paid off in full in less than two years.

The Washington Society for the Blind officially undertook its obligations of the vending stand program in the District of Columbia on September 1, 1939. At this time there were twelve stands in operation with others planned.

The growth of the vending stand program in the District of Columbia was rapid. There was never a financial problem as the program was entirely self-sufficient. This program became a model for other states to follow.

The fiscal year of the program coincided with the dates of the Federal fiscal year—July 1 through June 30. The following figures show the number of operators, average earnings of all operators, and the total number of stands during the fiscal years of 1958, 1963, 1968, and 1971.

In the fiscal year ending June 30, 1958, the total number of blind operators was 71; average earnings of all operators amounted to $4,970. Number of stands was 65.

In the fiscal year ending June 30, 1963, the total number of blind operators was 84. The average earnings per operator amounted to $7,932. The total number of stands was 75.

For the fiscal year ending June 30, 1968, the total number of blind operators was 84. The annual average earnings of operators was $10,020. The total number of stands was 72.

For the fiscal year ending June 30, 1971, which was the last year of my government career, the total number of blind operators was 81. The annual average earnings of operators amounted to $9,084. The total number of stands was 74.

The income from the vending machines which were considered a part of the vending stand in that particular Federal building, was added to the total income of each operator in question. In the latter years some of the Federal stand locations consisted of vending machines only, and the location in each case was manned by a blind operator, who was taught to load the machines and to make minor repairs to them.

An extensive training program was inaugurated from the very beginning of the vending stand program, and as the responsibilities became greater, the training was increased in intensity.

The following insert concerning the training of vending stand operators was furnished to me by William W. Thompson, coordinator, Vending Stand Program, Bureau of Rehabilitation Services for the District of Columbia:

Operator Training in the
Randolph-Sheppard Vending Stand Program
of Washington, D.C.

The training of vending stand operator candidates in Washington, D.C., is essentially on-the-job training. That is to say, that the program Training Center includes a vending stand whose patrons are the employees of a relatively small Federal agency. The training is conducted by personnel of the Bureau of Rehabilitation Services in the Social Rehabilitation Administration of the D.C. Department of Human Resources.

When a client is referred and accepted for training in the Vending Stand Program he has already completed pre-vocational rehabilitation or has otherwise demonstrated that he is prepared to deal with his life situation as a blind person. In screening potential vending stand trainees the Program Coordinator looks for individuals of at least average intelligence with the motivation in the capacity to accept the responsibility which comes with independent small business management. All training candidates are drawn from the caseload of the Bureau of Rehabilitation Services and the Vending Stand Program Coordinator works closely with the Bureau's Counselors regarding the referral and selection of clients for training. Instructions are given in both manual or "over-the-counter" vending and in automatic vending. The trainee proceeds at his own pace, there being no prescribed or set length of training. Instruction is continued until the trainee demonstrates proficiency in all aspects of basic vending stand operation or until it is demonstrated conclusively that he is unable to master these activities. The new trainee begins by observing a more experienced candidate assisting in the cleaning of the vending stand, learning the prices of merchandise, helping with the storage and display of merchandise and the like. As training proceeds he learns basic money handling procedures, the adding of sales, making change, paying bills, and the protection of vending stand funds. Training also, quite naturally, includes principles of merchandising, ordering stock, receiving and storing stock, displaying of merchandise, and overall, inventory control. Much stress is laid upon cleanliness and sanitation. Instructions are given in the rotation of stock to insure freshness, and to avoid sale of spoiled or stale items. Cleaning techniques are taught so that the totally blind trainee can be reasonably sure that the vending stand will always be clean and free of unsightly clutter. Relations with customers and with dealers are important and the trainee is helped to understand how efficiency and pleasantness in this area can add to the smoothness and productivity of vending stand operations. Specific instructions are given in making coffee, opening and serving heated soups and stews, heating sandwiches, and the like. This is also true in the area of automatic vending, where the trainee is taught to sanitize and load and otherwise service automatic vend-

83

ing equipment. In the training stand, hot beverages and soft drinks are vended automatically and the trainee learns to handle the servicing requirement of these machines. Also available in a work area of the Training Center are other types of automatic vending equipment such as cold food, pastry, and cigarette venders. These machines are not in active service, but the trainee learns their operation and servicing requirements on a "dummy" basis.

Specific instructions are also given in ways to differentiate merchandise by shape, size, packaging, etc. Trainees are also taught how to mark merchandise for future identification using braille felt tip markers and various other devices.

The percentage of the gross sales paid by the vending stand operators in the District of Columbia amounted to approximately 8 percent. This was known as the administrative levy. The Washington Society for the Blind entered into a contract with the Vocational Rehabilitation Service of the District of Columbia, the licensing agency, which spelled out specifically what each organization was obligated to do in this joint venture. The administrative levy provided sufficient funds to handle the enormous demand for vending stands in the Federal buildings, and the cooperation on the part of the Public Buildings Administration was very gratifying. A reserve and stabilization fund was set up to take care of unusual demands for new vending stand equipment. The society was permitted to take 10 percent of the administrative levy which it could use for other employment projects for blind persons. Two of the employment projects were blade sharpening and the manufacture of aluminum milk boxes which were sold to the various dairies in the area.

The District program also became famous because of its supervised controlled feature. Under this system, the vending stand operator did not own his stand. Upon his death or retirement, the stand location would be assigned to another blind person. This system enabled the stand operator to be promoted from one stand to another, thereby undertaking larger assignments with greater responsibilities, depending

84

upon his ability, and thus enabling him to earn more money, since he was entitled to all of the net earnings. Many of the states adopted this system which accounts for the rapid growth of the vending stand program from a national standpoint.

The procedure in licensing an operator was quite simple. The vending stand applicant would be selected by the Vocational Rehabilitation Service.

When a visually handicapped person became a vocational rehabilitation client, he would go through the diagnostic procedures to determine what his abilities were and the kind of employment he would be most likely to succeed in. A general medical examination would determine his physical ability. An ophthalmological examination would reveal whether sight restoration was possible, and if so, to what extent. A study would be made of his past educational and employment experience. A psychological test would enable the rehabilitation counselor to determine more easily the kind of training and job placement his client would be more successful with. After studying all of this diagnostic material, and if the counselor thought his client could make a success of the vending stand program, the client would be told about the program to determine whether he was interested in it. If the client wanted to undertake the vending stand work, he would be trained for this purpose. The training period would determine whether the client was really suited for vending stand work, and if he successfully completed this training, he would be assigned to one of the small stands. He would be carefully supervised during the first few months, and if he indicated that he could perform his duties as a vending stand operator, then he would be given a vending stand license as provided for in the Randolph-Sheppard Act.

From there on the stand operator would be practically on his own, except for periodic visits from his supervisor. Such a supervisor would be assigned some twelve or fourteen stands. In the District of Columbia it was comparatively easy for him to handle twelve or fourteen stands as all of them were within a three-mile radius.

To further illustrate the advantages of a supervised controlled vending stand program, a good example is the City Post Office stand.

In 1944, during World War II, the City Postmaster requested the installation of a vending stand under the authority of the Randolph-Sheppard Act as the employees within the building had no food service. The installation was arranged and equipped for a twenty-four-hours-per-day stand. Three visually handicapped operators were assigned to this location, each one taking a different eight-hour shift. When any new stand opened, the Washington Society for the Blind would run it for a two-month period to find out the kind of operation that location would require, and this would determine what operators within the program would best suit that particular location. This new location would mean the possibility of three promotion opportunities for three vending stand operators who had the required abilities.

The problem which came up with respect to this location was obtaining good equipment. Good materials because of the war were scarce and hard to obtain. After some priorities were obtained the stand was built and installed in about two months. Several years after the war was over, this location was reequipped with stainless steel counters and with all new fixtures at a cost of over thirty thousand dollars. The three operators assigned there at the beginning were still there, and the entire expense for the work did not cost these operators anything. The administrative levy and the reserve and stabilization fund took care of everything.

The first visually impaired person assigned to the vending stand program in the District of Columbia was Earl Richardson. He assumed his duties during the first week in January of 1938. I had met Mr. Richardson at a summer outing during the month of July in 1937. He told me of his family situation which consisted of his wife, two children, and an aunt, all trying to live on a welfare grant of $135 a month. He had not been employed for some time. Although he had a little sight, it was insufficient for him to take on most kinds of work. He knew that the vending stand program would be ideal for him. He had a pleasing personality, and it seemed to me that he would be successful with such an opportunity. He also knew that he was one of many candidates for vending stand opportunities within the District. He was directed to Mr. Clunk's office soon after Mr. Clunk began his duties, and it turned out that Mr. Richardson became the first operator assigned to the program.

In 1942, Mr. Richardson had been promoted to a larger stand in the Lemon Building. Because of the war, this building was utilized around the clock, and Mr. Richardson's stand had to be enlarged and equipped to take on the added load. He put in long hours and was able to hire competent help to enable him to conduct the entire operation himself. Since he had the ability, there was no problem. I want to point out in his case that he was able to earn $14,000 the first year of his enlarged vending stand opportunity. This is all a part of the public record, and Mr. Richardson's kind of success story can be told many times in the case of other vending stand operators in the District of Columbia.

Another interesting account is one which involved Clyde Hooks. In 1940 I had been assigned to do casework with the District Office of Vocational Rehabilitation Service. When I returned from lunch one day, I was told that Mr. Hooks had been in to see me. He had come without an appointment and he could not wait until I returned. He had been referred to my office by the Bureau of Workmen's Compensation. Since he left his address and telephone number, I arranged to see him the following day. He was a man in his early thirties, married, and had three children. When I visited him, he and his family had given up their apartment and moved in with his mother-in-law. Mr. Hooks, some three months before, had lost all of his sight due to an accident while at work. He was employed as an iron worker and the machine he worked on came apart and part of it hit him between the eyes. His main concern was what our office could suggest for him to do in order to earn a living for his family. The job he was on paid twenty-eight dollars a week and he used to earn eight dollars a week from a vegetable stand he ran over the weekends with another person. As he was highly motivated and completely recovered from his accident, and having a dynamic personality, I immediately forgot routine procedures and told him about the vending stand program. I felt he was in great need of a boost at once before anxiety took over. I recall how he and his wife were so elated with the prospect of a vending stand, and I assured him that we could process his case at once and within two weeks got him started with his training. I knew he and his family were living in crowded quarters under the circumstances, and I also told him that after he got his vending stand license I could work out an arrangement with the Bureau of Compensation and have part of his disability compensation released for a down payment on a house.

It all worked out just as I had predicted. Mr. Hooks learned to travel from his home to the training stand, and in less than one month he was ready to be put on a vending stand to which he was licensed. He took over the stand at the D.C. General Hospital, and his earnings the first year amounted to five thousand dollars.

It was very easy for me to arrange with the Compensation Bureau to release $2,500 to Mr. Hooks for the down payment on a house in a very fine section of the city which he bought for $9,700. Mr. Hooks is now retired and lives in North Carolina. When he retired from the program in 1971, he had no difficulty in selling his house at approximately $23,000.

Thus, the self-supporting and supervised controlled vending stand program in the District of Columbia grew and thrived, as the figures in this chapter reveal, and despair and helplessness turned into new lives and aspirations for scores of blind persons.

During the time when the vending stand program in the District of Columbia was being launched, the Federal department in charge of the Randolph-Sheppard Act was also giving attention to the various state programs. State plans together with their guidelines were sent to all the states, and as soon as they were returned in proper shape, the licensing agency in each one was determined and approved. But there was not a great deal of progress in many states at the outset. This was due to the lack of funds for vending stand equipment and initial stocks of merchandise which had to be furnished to each blind vending stand operator.

In 1943, a new chapter was written in the field of work for the blind with the passage of the Barden-LaFollette Act which became a law on July 6, 1943, and which amended the Vocational Rehabilitation Act of 1920. These amendments represent the first comprehensive rehabilitation program for the blind. They have been hailed by many as the Magna Carta of the blind.

The Vocational Rehabilitation Act Amendments of 1943 (the Barden-LaFollette Act) radically changed the vocational rehabilitation concept in terms of (1) authorized services and (2) clients eligible for service. First, they provided that a vocational rehabilitation client could be furnished any service necessary to realize his full employment potential. Federal funds were made available to provide handicapped clients with the medical, surgical and other physical restoration services required to eradicate or alleviate their disabilities. The authorized services included surgery and therapeutic treatment, hospitalization, transportation, occupational licenses, tools and equipment, prosthetic devices, maintenance during training, and training equipment. Secondly, vocational rehabilitation services were extended to the mentally ill and mentally retarded persons. Additionally, the Vocational Rehabilitation Act Amendments of 1943 provided for greater financial participation on the part of the Federal government.

It is quite obvious from provisions of the Barden-LaFollette Act that for the first time the various states had money to really start and expand their vending stand programs, along with their other vocational rehabilitation services to the blind and other physically handicapped clients. The provision for "tools and equipment" provided funds for stand equipment and the initial stocks of merchandise. And with greater Federal participation in the state programs, more Federal money was available for expansion of state programs of a varied nature.

In order to show the growth of the vending stand program, I have taken some figures from the official fiscal reports of the vending stand program prepared by the Department of Health, Education and Welfare, Office of Vocational Rehabilitation. For this illustration I am using the states of New York, Pennsylvania, Maryland, Ohio, Illinois, and California. The table with its appropriate headings, follows:

Selected Data on Vending Stand Program

Fiscal Year Ending June 30	Total No. of Stands	Total No. of Blind Operators	Annual Average Earnings of Operators
NEW YORK			
1958	107	112	$ 3,507
1963	112	124	4,464
1968	121	146	5,784
1972	139	167	6,288
PENNSYLVANIA			
1958	78	78	3,990
1963	131	135	5,160
1968	187	187	6,300
1972	194	194	7,248

MARYLAND

1958	27	27	4,380
1963	43	43	7,020
1968	55	55	9,552
1972	78	71	12,072

OHIO

1958	84	86	3,167
1963	131	131	5,856
1968	157	164	5,436
1972	182	192	7,128

ILLINOIS

1958	63	63	3,786
1963	68	68	4,932
1968	83	89	6,408
1972	87	84	8,904

CALIFORNIA

1958	174	186	4,086
1963	225	231	5,952
1968	277	284	7,044
1972	296	308	8,460

Chapter 10

Blind Persons in Federal Jobs

As mentioned in a previous chapter, the Randolph-Sheppard Act made it possible for blind persons to be employed by the Federal government. It made it mandatory that 50 percent of the personnel administering the act be blind. Although Joseph Clunk was the first blind person in Federal service, he used to say that he was the only one who would admit it. It was always a pleasure to work with him, for there was never a dull moment.

Soon after my assignment to work with the District of Columbia Vocational Rehabilitation Service in 1940, where the major part of my duties was to find employment for blind persons other than the vending stand program, I was visited by a young lady, Miss Edith Ford, who was trying to hold down a bundle wrapping job with one of the large department stores. Miss Ford was legally blind, and had graduated from high school in June of that year. She told me that her eyesight was so bad that it was difficult for her to read the handwriting on the order slips, and she knew that she could not last much longer in that job. She had taken typing at high school, and when I told her how successful totally blind persons were in typing jobs by using a transcribing machine, such as the Dictaphone, she became very much interested in being further trained so that she could qualify as a transcribing machine operator with some Federal government agency.

When Mr. Clunk's office was set up, one of the first things done was to arrange with the United States Civil Service Commission for a typing test for blind persons and establish a Blind Typist Register. When this was accomplished, this register was used to select a blind typist to work in Mr. Clunk's office.

Miss Ford did not take the test as she was still in high school, but I did not think I would encounter any difficulty placing her with some Federal agency once I got her trained. I opened her case and processed it in the usual manner, and arranged for her to take her training at night after working hours as she could not afford to be without employment. She was only earning seventeen dollars a week at the time, but that was important.

After about two months in a refresher course of typing, Miss Ford proved that she was very capable, and she learned to use the transcribing machine along with the typewriter.

At that time the War Department was in great need of typists. World War II had brought about an intensive preparedness program. I was able to reach the personnel director of the War Department on the telephone, and he set up an appointment for me to see him personally. He did not know at the time that the client I wanted to see him about was legally blind. I recall it was not difficult for me to sell him on the idea of hiring a blind typist, but he pointed out to me that such a person, who was not on a special kind of register, could not be hired by any Federal government agency because she did not have the physical requirements for Federal government employment. He told me that the physical requirement for eyesight was that all applicants for Federal jobs had to have a visual acuity in the better eye with correction of twenty over thirty, even though the other eye might be entirely blind. He was sympathetic, but there was nothing he could do about it.

When I returned to my office, I discussed the matter with

my chief. He gave me permission to do whatever I could to get the rules changed.

The next day I put in a telephone call to Mrs. Lucille Foster McMillan, chairman of the U.S. Civil Service Commission. Mrs. McMillan's husband had at one time been governor of Tennessee, and since I was a native of Tennessee, Mrs. McMillan was only too glad to see me personally, especially since she was very much interested in the employment problems of blind persons.

I recall that when I related the story of Edith Ford and my turndown at the War Department due to the physical requirements rule, she got into high gear at once. She called a Mr. Hull to her office. He was a high ranking administrative officer, and she told him about the Edith Ford case. Before he left her office she suggested that a meeting be set up within a week to which would be invited certain persons of the Federal Division of Rehabilitation and my chief from the District Rehabilitation Service, and anyone else who wished to come who might be interested.

The meeting came about the following week. There were about twelve persons in attendance. Mr. Hull was also on hand and also the new U.S. Civil Service Commission medical director, Dr. Vernon K. Harvey. I related the Edith Ford story again briefly. The Vocational Rehabilitation staff people got in some licks by telling Mrs. McMillan how difficult it was to obtain Federal jobs for physically handicapped persons other than the blind. Mrs. McMillan was very much impressed, and promised that something would be done about it at once. She assured me that I would not have any difficulty in the not so distant future with my blind clients.

When the meeting was over, Dr. Harvey came over to me and told me he would cooperate with us. He had just come from Indiana where he had done some medical work for the vocational rehabilitation agency of that state.

Not long after that meeting, I was able to obtain a transcribing machine job for Miss Ford with the Works Progress

94

Administration. She more than proved her ability to do her work there. She made a career with the Federal government, as many years later she contacted me for some information and she was with a government agency at that time.

To show his interest and cooperation with us, Dr. Harvey set up weekly meetings in his office at which members of the staffs of the Federal and District Vocational Rehabilitation offices were in attendance. These conferences led to changes in the physical requirements for many Federal jobs, thus making it possible to get appointments for more physically handicapped persons.

One day, at one of these meetings, Dr. Harvey opened the meeting by telling us he had a good case to relate to us which would show how cooperative the U.S. Civil Service Commission was in the employment of the physically handicapped. He told us he had recently gotten a call from one of the professional workers at the D.C. Employment Service who told him that he understood the Federal government was having difficulty hiring capable telephone switchboard operators. Dr. Harvey assured him that he was correct. And then this Employment Service worker went on to tell him that he had a young lady who would make an excellent telephone switchboard operator, but that she did not have any arms. Dr. Harvey thought at first this was a joke, and asked the caller what he really had called about. The caller convinced Dr. Harvey that he had such an armless switchboard operator, and he was prepared to have her show him how she operated the switchboard with her toes. Dr. Harvey told us he went down to witness the demonstration, and this young lady had proved her ability beyond any doubt. She was hired the next day and placed on the job as a switchboard operator at the Mount Alto Hospital on Wisconsin Avenue, N.W., which was a veterans' facility.

This young switchboard operator had come from North Carolina where she had attended one of the colleges there. She was Miss Grace Hopper, and she remained on that same job for sixteen years. I later came to know her personally as she and I were very active with the Nation's Capital Chapter of the National Association of the Physically Handicapped. We would attend luncheons of interest to the physically handicapped, and she had no trouble eating her meals or lighting a cigarette with her "educated" toes. When the vending stand operators of the District gave me a testimonial dinner some years ago, I invited Grace and her husband to be my special guests and they were seated at the head table. She is happily married to Ross Cleaves and has been for some time, and she still has that dynamic personality and charm which would be the envy of any woman.

I called Grace Cleaves recently to verify the facts of this story and to get her permission to use it, and when I called her, she, as usual, answered the telephone.

The important lesson to be learned from this Grace Cleaves story is to point out that all physically handicapped persons are normal individuals and they all want to be accepted by society as such. They are not equal to other persons with respect to their physical makeup, but they learn to overcome their physical deficiencies and conduct themselves quite normally and adequately in the fulfillment of their social and employment obligations.

I was at my office when, on one occasion, Dr. Harvey called me and said he would like to come up and have a talk with me. He wanted me to recommend to him a capable blind young lady who was a skilled typist, as he would employ her in his office. He told me if she worked out satisfactorily, he would be able to sell the idea to other Federal government offices. I had just placed such a person with the Library of Congress, and when I told her of Dr. Harvey's visit, she gladly went for an interview as she was anxious to be able to help other blind women get typing jobs with the Federal government. It so happened that she was an excellent employee, and before many months went by, I had run out of capable transcribing machine employee candidates.

With the onset of World War II involving the United States, many blind persons came to Washington to accept government positions, having been sent there by their own vocational rehabilitation departments. What we had worked out in Washington for the blind had benefited blind persons throughout the nation insofar as getting jobs with the Federal government was concerned.

In a recent study made by the Bureau of Recruiting and Examining of the United States Civil Service Commission, it is shown that there are fifty different categories of Federal jobs in which the blind are employed. Some of the job titles are Dark Room Aid, Educational Therapist, Electrical Equipment Repairer Helper, Health Technician, Industrial Shop Worker, Information Receptionist, Laboratory Helper, Medical Radio Technician, Meteorologist, Ordnance Equipment Mechanic, and Radiological Film Processor.

The following story tells of my experience with McKinley Young, Jr., who was recommended to my office in 1953 by the National Institutes of Health, Bethesda, Maryland, where Mr. McKinley had gone from his home in North Carolina to ascertain if this Federal government medical research facility could restore his sight. I recall when he first came to my office. He knew then that he would always be without sight, but he had his spirit and determination to succeed with any employment undertaking we might work out for him as a blind person. As he was a high school graduate, I recommended to him that he learn to type and become a transcribing machine operator as there was a big demand for such employees at that time. I sent him to a training facility where, after four months, he was able to take the Civil Service typing test. He passed with flying colors, and I was able to place him with the Civil Service Commission. While employed with the commission, he received four superior performance cash awards and a citation from the District of Columbia Board of Commissioners. He then was transferred to the Veterans Administration, Board of Veterans Appeals in 1962. With the latter office, Mr. Young received five superior performance cash awards. He was on this job for several years when he again came to my office and told me that he had gone about as far as he could with the Veterans Administration as a

McKinley Young with the Data Processing Center,
Veterans Administration, Austin, Texas.

transcriber. Since he was such a marvelous worker, with plenty on the ball, I told him I would see if the Veterans Administration would be interested in getting him trained as a computer programmer. My vocational rehabilitation office would pay for the training if the Veterans Administration was interested. I contacted the V.A. personnel, and they were very much interested in the possibility. Since there was a special course for the blind in computer programming to start in less than a week, the V.A. had a lot of things to do to see if Mr. Young could fit into their computer programming division in Austin, Texas, where Mr. Young and his wife had agreed to go if Mr. Young could be successfully trained. It so happened that all of the information was received in four days, and on the fifth day he started his training with this special class of blind persons. In eight months he was graduated at the top of his class. I asked Mr. Young, for the purpose of this book, to describe for me how he conducts his work as a computer programmer, and he sent me the following:

This letter is in reply to your request that I forward information to you concerning the devices and aids I use as a computer programmer. I am presently working with a project which has a large number of project assignments which must be completed in a very short period of time. It has been necessary for most of us to work, at least part of, seven days per week. For that reason I am late answering your letter.

A brief summary of the methods, techniques, devices, and aids which I use as a computer programmer is as follows: When I receive a new project assignment, the job specifications are read into a tape recorder, which I then transcribe in braille. After a careful study of the specifications, I discuss any possible errors of omission or commission, or any areas which might need additional explanation with the author of the specifications. Next I prepare a narrative-type flow chart in braille or by using a set of specially designed flow chart symbols (it consists of a number of dies, each of which contains a flow chart symbol engraved on it; the dies are similar to those used for making notary seals) to plan the method I will use to satisfy job specifications. I then write the necessary program instructions in braille. I then use a typewriter with a piece of bond paper, using columnal tab sets, I type the program instructions in preparation for submission to the keypunch section. When the keypunched cards are returned to me, I desk check each card to verify its correctness by using a card reader (this is a device into which an IBM punched card can fit; it is constructed in such a way that using a stylus one can verify the correctness of the punches in each column). If any errors are found, I use a portable keypunch machine and punch a corrected card for each one in error. I then submit my job to operations to be run on the computer. The output from my job is then run through a braille conversion program which converts English to a braille format. A braille printout is obtained merely by taping a piece of ordinary elastic across the print bar. I study

99

the braille listing and if any errors are found I repeat the above steps until the job is certified by our audit staff as meeting all specifications. With some minor modifications, most blind programmers follow the steps I have set forth.

If I can furnish any further information or further describe the above, please do not fail to let me know.

Another interesting government employee, who is a transcribing machine operator, is Jean Dorf, who is presently employed at the Department of Justice. Mr. Dorf sent me a description of his work and a brief history of his employment

Jean Dorf with the Department of Justice, Washington, D.C.

record, but he was too modest to insert that he, as an employee for the Veterans Administration and for the Department of Justice, received many awards for outstanding service. He is very active in the community, and last year he was the President of the District of Columbia Association of Workers for the Blind, which organization does a great deal of philanthropic work on behalf of blind persons in the community. His story follows:

Transcriber's Progress

by Jean Dorf

When I first took the transcribing course—in the mid-thirties—dictation was taken from a Dictaphone machine using the wax cylinders and transcription was done on a manual standard typewriter. Because of my not having any reading vision, my work had to be proofread for typographical errors. Along with taking dictation from the Dictaphone, my instruction included learning Braille shorthand, enabling me to take verbal dictation and reproduce my notes on a standard typewriter.

My first job in the business world was taking dictation verbally and transcribing the material on a standard typewriter.

In 1950 I was fortunate in getting a position with the Federal government in the Veterans Administration, at which time I was introduced to the electric typewriter. This made transcription faster and much less tiring. During the ensuing years material was taken from various types of dictating equipment and transcribed on an IBM electric typewriter.

In mid-1969, after I had been with the Department of Justice since January 1964, I was introduced to the IBM Magnetic Tape Selectric Typewriter, at which I am seated in the accompanying photograph. This machine operates just like a regular typewriter, but while typing the material onto paper, the work is simultaneously recorded onto a magnetic tape. In this way, one can correct errors while typing simply by backspacing and striking the right character or characters. In this way the tape is corrected. Upon completion of a piece of material, a fresh sheet of paper can be inserted into the typewriter and by setting the machine in proper operation, a perfect copy can be run off.

In addition, if errors are made without realization, they can be corrected by inserting another sheet of paper and stopping the machine at a given point.

Therefore, in the years that I have been working as a transcriber, progress has been made from typing on a standard manual typewriter to that of using the IBM MT/ST on which a blind person can correct his own errors. In addition, the transcribing machines have gone from the old wax cylinders to magnetic belts that can be erased and reused many times over again.

Another very outstanding Federal government employee was Charles R. Simpson who joined the Internal Revenue Service in 1952. He was an expert in tax law, and in 1965 his ability in this field was recognized by President Lyndon B. Johnson who nominated him as judge of the Tax Court of the United States. His background is so impressive that I will include the following biographical sketch of him:

Charles R. Simpson was born in Danville, Illinois, June 16, 1921, and is married to Ruth V. Simpson.

He received his B.A. degree with highest honors from the University of Illinois in 1944. In 1945, he received his J.D. degree with high honors from the University of Illinois College of Law. He was elected to Phi Beta Kappa, Phi Kappa Phi, and the Order of the Coif, and was president of the Student Bar Association.

He was admitted to the Illinois Bar in 1945 and was in the private practice of law in Champaign, Illinois, from 1946 to 1949. He was elected a member of the Illinois General Assembly in 1946 and served two terms from 1947 through 1950. During this period, he was chairman of the Champaign County Chapter of the National Foundation for Infantile Paralysis. In 1949, he was awarded a fellowship to do graduate work at the Harvard Law School and received his LL.M. in 1950. He served as a teaching fellow at Harvard the school year of 1950-51.

In July 1951, he joined the staff of the Office of Price Stabilization. In October 1952, he transferred to the Internal Revenue Service, Office of Chief Counsel, Legislation and Regulations Division, where he served as an attorney from 1952 to 1957; special assistant to the director, 1957-1959; staff assistant to the chief counsel, 1959-1961; chief, Special Income Tax Branch, 1961; assistant director, November 1961-April 1964; and as director from April 1964 to September 2, 1965.

On March 29, 1965, he received a Meritorious Service Award from Secretary of the Treasury Dillon. On May 26, 1965, he was selected to receive the Justice Tom C. Clark Award as the outstanding government career attorney for 1964.

President Johnson announced his nomination as a judge of the Tax Court of the United States on August 19, 1965, and he was sworn in at the White House on September 2, 1965.

On November 21, 1968, he received the Federal Tax Forum of New York City Award for distinguished service in the tax field.

On May 5, 1969, he received the Tax Society of New York University Achievement Award.

Judge Simpson is a member of the American Bar Association and also a member of the Tax Section, the American Judicature Society, and of the American Law Institute.

The United States Civil Service Commission has performed an excellent public relations job in bringing to the forefront each year ten outstanding Federal employees who are physically handicapped. The Outstanding Handicapped Federal Employee of the Year Award was first conceived by the Interagency Advisory Group Committee on Selective Placement Programs. The fourteen members of this particular IAG committee envisioned an annual award program which would focus attention on the job capabilities of those handicapped persons already employed by the Federal government. This generally increases awareness of their valuable contributions, publicizes Federal career opportunities available to other handicapped persons, and perhaps most importantly, offers still more evidence that the handicapped are able to perform top-quality work—both in government and private industry.

The Civil Service Commission formally established this new nationwide recognition program in October 1968, making the criterion "exceptional job performance . . . in spite of severely limiting physical factors." Ten finalists are selected each year from handicapped employees nominated by Federal departments and agencies with the winner being named at a special ceremony honoring the ten finalists.

In 1969, one of the ten finalists was Miss Magdalene Phillips. In the printed program of that year, the following was written about Miss Phillips:

Miss Magdalene Phillips was born in Baker, Oregon. She has been totally blind since early adulthood but, like most handi-

103

Magdalene Phillips with Letterman Army Hospital, San Francisco, California.

capped employees, she far exceeds the job performance standards for the position she occupies.

Miss Phillips has spent the last three years as a dictating machine transcriber at Letterman Army Hospital in San Francisco. She has developed an almost uncanny accuracy in the transcription of detailed reports bristling with complex surgical and other medical terminology. She handles dictation from six different medical officers and her skills are such that she is able to switch smoothly from one style of dictation to another while maintaining a very high quality of work.

Refusing to be preoccupied with her own problems, Miss Phillips unselfishly gives of herself and her time. During lunch breaks and before and after working hours she counsels newly blinded patients entering the hospital. Her quiet, cheerful, and reassuring manner have helped to encourage these patients to work hard at the task of rehabilitation.

She was the recipient of a national award from the Shell Oil Company for her participation in a Traffic Commission Safety Program in which she traveled extensively over a four-year period—instructing between 60,000 and 70,000 children on the subject of traffic safety.

104

In 1971 one of the ten finalists was Dr. Bernard A. Perella. In the printed program for that year, the following was written about Dr. Perella:

Bernard Perella, a native of West Chester, Pennsylvania, has been blind since the age of five. At the age of 23, in 1963, he received a Bachelor of Science degree from Villanova University, with a major in mathematics and a minor in physics. The years between these two ages of this man represented a great deal of courageous effort.

He was hired by NSA in 1963 and, since 1966, has been at the Mathematical Research Division, Office of Research, where he is a GS-13 Mathematician/Computer Programmer. He designed a special program to convert ADP data to Braille, thus establishing an effective communications link between himself and his agency's computers. His computer "language" is being mass produced by IBM for use by other blind programmers. Dr. Perella was recently selected by the National Braille Authority to serve on its subcommittee on computer Braille codes.

He has made many important contributions to the solution of difficult and highly classified problems at NSA—both by brilliant computer programming and by providing sharp insights and ideas. He is now exploring techniques that would permit a blind person to use computer remote terminals in spite of that equipment's visually-oriented cathode ray tubes. He is trying to devise an audio signal system for these terminal units.

Dr. Perella requires almost no assistance that he cannot already provide for himself if necessary. He does occasionally have a document read to him, but usually only once. He has a phenomenal memory, moves about streets and buildings using only his lightweight, sensing cane, and routinely travels by himself throughout the country to attend meetings of professional societies or to carry out some government assignment. He does all of this with ease, making full use of all the advantages of modern technology. His experiences in general are reminiscent of a statement once made by Michael Dunn, the famous Irish actor who happened to be born a dwarf. He said he viewed sophisticated machinery as an extension of himself and he uses all sorts of mechanized and transistorized equipment to make his life easier and himself more efficient.

In my many years of government employment, I found the Internal Revenue Service to be most cooperative in the place-

Dr. Bernard A. Perella, Outstanding Handicapped Employee of the National Security Agency for the year 1971, is shown here receiving a citation from Mrs. Tricia Nixon Cox and Mrs. Jane Baker Spain, vice-chairman, Civil Service Commission.

ment of many of my blind clients. Nicholas W. Williams, coordinator for the Employment of the Handicapped, and connected with the Personnel Department of IRS, was in close touch with me during the early stages of the Taxpayer Service Representative project. Mr. Williams was kind enough to send me the following article written by him titled, "The Internal Revenue Service and the Blind":

A New Concept

It all started in late 1966 and early 1967, when Fred Johnson, then the Little Rock, Arkansas District Director of the Internal Revenue Service, conceived the idea that the blind might very well serve as Taxpayer Service Representatives (answering taxpayers' inquiries over the phone).

Fred asked a very simple question, "Why couldn't a blind person serve as a 'TSR' as well as the sighted?" His forecast proved accurate. As the result, in 1973 over 75 blind persons in 38 states perform very satisfactorily as "TSR's." Most of the thousands of taxpayers who "call in" from Maine to California are not aware that they are directing their inquiries to blind persons who are able to locate their calls on the incoming board. By means of a light probe (a simple electronic device), held in one hand, he senses the light flashes and thus knows where to press the flashing button to take the incoming call.

Taxpayer Service Representatives

After a series of conferences in 1967, in Little Rock and Washington, attended by representatives of the Rehabilitation Services Administration (Dr. Douglas MacFarland, Director, Office of the Blind, and George Magers, Assistant Director), Arkansas Enterprises for the Blind (Roy Kumpe, Executive Director) and the Treasury Department (the late Allen F. Marshall, Assistant Director, Employment, Treasury), Fred Johnson and Nicholas W. Williams (Coordinator for the Employment of the Handicapped), of the Internal Revenue Service, things really started to move.

In March 1967, a one-year pilot program was approved for training "TSR's" at AEB. This was followed by a three-year HEW grant also to AEB. The three-year demonstration was called "Training 50 Blind Persons to Work as Tax Assisters for the Internal Revenue Service." The two projects lasted from March 1967 through May 1971 during which period the "TSR's" were trained at no cost to the Revenue Service.

AEB and Training

The Arkansas Enterprises for the Blind continues to train most of the Revenue Service "TSR's" even though the grant has run out and the several State Rehabilitation Services now finance the training. Usually applicants for training must have been priorly screened by the Revenue officials to determine that they possess "meet and deal" qualities to deal with taxpayers.

Dr. Allan L. Ward, AEB's Director of Research and Staff Development, and Elmo A. Knoch, Jr., its Director of Training, wrote an article for *New Outlook*, March 1972, "Training Blind Persons to Work as Taxpayer Service Representatives." They summed the evaluation and training programs as follows:

> Individuals referred for "TSR" training are recommended for such training on the basis of the results of a 30-day period of evaluation. The evaluation criteria involve the skills considered necessary for success as a "TSR." These include mental ability (IQ, memory, vocabulary, etc.), mobility, independent living, communications (braille, handwriting, typewriting, telephone skills, mathematics, recording equipment), and availability for employment. Where indicated, it may be recommended that individuals be referred for additional personal adjustment prevocational training.
>
> The 15-week course of instruction, which has a schedule kept flexible enough to meet the needs of the individual trainee, includes the following: introduction and the income tax—eight weeks; employment and excise taxes—five weeks; automatic data processing—one week; other taxes, exempt organizations, and departing aliens—one day; administrative provisions—one day; guest speakers—three days. Incorporated within the schedule is a program of weekly written tests and shorter quizzes, both written and oral. The course also includes role-playing sessions which are often recorded on tape for play-back and critical comment.

A One Day Trip

Billy J. Brown, Director, Personnel Division, upon occasion of his January 30, 1973, visit to the Arkansas Enterprises for the Blind and to the Little Rock IRS District, participated in the ceremony marking the 100th "TSR" graduate at AEB and prophetically said that he looked forward to the next 100 "TSR's" during the 1970's. Actually, 16 classes have graduated 111 persons; lots were drawn from the January 1973 class to determine who would be honored as the 100th graduate. Penny Keim, of Tennessee, was selected.

Jack McSpadden, employed at the IRS District Office since 1967, was the first to graduate from the training program at AEB and is symbolic of high achievement in this unusually successful program.

Initially, logistics wise (brailling, tapes, and visual aids), the IRS depended upon the voluntary service of the Library of Congress, the American Red Cross, and the American Printing House for the Blind. Now IRS has its own budget for the blind.

Braille Production and Sensory Aids Testing

During the past year and six months, the IRS program for supplying materials required by blind employees of the Service has undergone several major changes. While this effort has concentrated on the particular needs of blind "TSR's," its advances may result in improved services for many other blind people as well.

The need for large amounts of brailled material, in short periods of time, forced the Service into looking at new production methods and alternatives to commercial braille. The first change to the braille production procedure included editing and reformating information in order to reduce the number of pages required to translate from the printed original (this also resulted in readability). The next and most important change to our program came in the form of computerized generation of braille. Beginning with the 1972 edition of *Your Federal Income Tax, Publication 17*, IRS expanded this computer effort to include the *1973 Income Tax Tables, Tax Guide for Small Business, Publication 334*, and thirty-four Taxpayer Information Publications. Computer generated braille now accounts for approximately 85% of all braille purchased by the Service. Editing, reformation, and computerization has allowed the Service to expand from 150,000 to 750,000 pages of braille produced annually, while improving quality, speeding up delivery schedules, and reducing the cost per brailled page.

Another significant development is the initial production of large type (18-point) material for partially sighted employees. This, like the computer generated braille, is produced by making use of the magnetic tapes that are prepared for electronic composition of the public-use printed editions of the *Tax Guide for*

Small Business and Taxpayer Information Publications. The fact that these tapes are already available allows IRS to keep braille costs down and produce large type material at a very low cost.

To augment the advances made in braille and large type production, the Service has been involved in two test projects of sensory aids, jointly with Taxpayer Service Division. On February 4, 1972, it requested a test installation of a braille printer and Taxpayer Service Division responded by placing one in the Little Rock District Office. This braille printer installation has proved that it is possible to produce quality braille in the offices that could either translate IDRS information or give us the ability to produce virtually any braille material required by a blind "TSR." On June 13, 1972, a second test proposal was made to Taxpayer Service Division, and it again responded by working and putting together an extensive field test of a direct reading machine for the blind. The Optacon is an optical scanner which converts the printed page into tactile images and gives blind people access to ink print material which has been unavailable in the past. While both of these projects are still in test status, they appear to present solutions to problems faced by many employed blind people in the past.

By Leaps and Bounds

The program has grown by leaps and bounds. On February 10, 1972, Commissioner Johnnie M. Walters wrote to all of his Assistant Commissioners, Regional Commissioners, District, Service Center and IRS Data Center Directors. He entitled it "Study in Courage and Achievement." It says:

> Those of us who have sight marvel at how many blind workers excel. The success of our blind Taxpayer Service Representatives is indeed a study in courage and achievement. We now have 70 blind Taxpayer Service Representatives who are living proof that being blind need not be a barrier to employment. Nor should we forget the sighted who took that extra step to employ the blind. Thus the blind and the sighted proved their mettle.
>
> In a sense, it is a fulfilment of a sort of American dream and proof that the Revenue Service does have a soul. I commend all of you, blind and sighted, who have achieved this success and encourage you to pursue your course with renewed vigor.

110

Again, sincere congratulations! My hope is that we may all grow in stature and continue successfully throughout the coming years to keep our employment of the blind very much alive and well.

Our goal still stands: at least one blind Taxpayer Service Representative in each major office.

The IRS Thrust

The IRS thrust is simply to get good people to work for the Service. While "TSR's" comprise the majority of its blind, many other blind persons perform with equal success: Attorneys, Tax Law Specialists, Typists, Economists, Computer Programmers and others. The Revenue Service's search is for excellence; this involves combating the misconceptions and convincing managers that the blind can perform in about any position as well or better than a sighted person. The Taxpayer Service Representative has gained the most attention but much remains to be done in other occupations and professions.

The Look Ahead

The "TSR" influence has been widespread and the Social Security Administration and the Civil Service Commission have embarked on similar types of information programs. There have also been inquiries from the British and Canadian governments about the possibility of establishing Taxpayer Service Representative programs in their countries.

More and more, both the private sector and government are realizing that involvement in other than everyday work situations is a prerequisite for self and/or corporate realization, . . . what John Gardner calls self-renewal. More and more in today's social upheaval, the goals of business and government include not just profit, but also the enhancing of the quality of life for everyone. The blind excel in the Revenue's world of work.

Mary Switzer

The late Mary Switzer, Administrator for Rehabilitation Services Administration, keynoted the 1969 all agency NBC-sponsored Washington Conference on the Employment of the Blind. At that time, she very simply and eloquently complimented IRS for "wisdom, imagination and understanding in breaking down barriers and moving ahead in providing opportunities for the

111

blind." The challenge remains in the days and years ahead for men of goodwill wherever they are. Past is but prologue.

The Outstanding Handicapped Federal Employee of the Year Award for 1973 took place at the Department of Commerce Building on April 5, 1973. Among the ten finalists were three blind persons. One was Jack O. McSpadden of Little Rock, Arkansas, a taxpayer service representative. The following is an excerpt from the program concerning Mr. McSpadden:

Jack O. McSpadden, taxpayer service representative with the
Internal Revenue Service, Little Rock, Arkansas.

Mr. McSpadden attended the Arkansas School for the Blind, graduating in 1961 as salutatorian of his class. Through the good offices of the Arkansas Rehabilitation Service for the Blind, he went on to graduate from Arkansas State College in 1966. He went to work for the Internal Revenue Service in July 1967, after completing a four-month training course at the Arkansas Enterprises for the Blind. Mr. McSpadden answers hundreds of telephone inquiries daily from taxpayers seeking help. Often the taxpayer's first and only contact with an IRS employee is with a person in Mr. McSpadden's position. His job requires special skills—tact, patience, and an expert knowledge of the tax code.

Another one of the ten finalists was Mrs. Assunta Lilley of Saint Louis, Missouri, who is a dictating machine transcriber with the United States Civil Service Commission. The program stated that Mrs. Lilley, being legally blind, has earned many awards and other kinds of recognition for her consistently high-quality work. She received Sustained Superior Performance Awards in 1957 and again in 1959; a beneficial suggestion cash award in 1960; a Group Performance Award in 1960; another beneficial suggestion payment in 1970, and, this year, a Special Achievement Award.

The winner of the ten finalists was Irvin Hershowitz of Washington, D.C., who is an employee of the Department of the Air Force, Bolling Air Force Base, Washington, D.C.

The program had the following to say about Mr. Hershowitz:

Irvin Hershowitz is an electronics whiz. He is an expert radio repairman, a first-class telephone trouble-shooter and, when necessary, he can serve as a skilled automobile mechanic. He is totally blind.

To cope with the electrical shock hazards inherent in his profession, Mr. Hershowitz developed an audio, tone-producing system to replace the usual color-coded wiring system used in electronics repair shops. He perfected this new design on his own time, and he used his personal funds to purchase the testing equipment which he converted to his tone system. This man's innovations don't stop there either. During his thirty years' Federal service, Irvin has translated into braille, (again on his own time) all technical manuals and other such materials pertaining to each of his two widely differing Federal occupations—radio repairman with the Aircraft Radio and Electronics Shop at Bolling Air Force Base, and telephone repairman, his present job with the Bolling Air Force Base Communications Group.

Mr. Hershowitz's list of awards is quite extensive. In addition to

Irvin Hershowitz, the Outstanding Handicapped Federal Employee of the Year 1973, receives his award plaque from Mrs. Julie Nixon Eisenhower. He is a telephone repairman at Bolling Air Force Base, Washington, D.C.

his repeated superior performances citations, his ideas for improved technical and safety methods have brought him numerous beneficial suggestion awards. His achievements have been publicized locally and nationally in dozens of newspaper and magazine articles, thus helping to remind people of the fact that the handicapped can do virtually anything if given the chance.

Chapter 11

The Non-Federal Blind Worker

With the passage of the Barden-LaFollette Act in 1943, as mentioned in Chapter 9, services to the blind received a new impetus in America with the inclusion of the State-Federal vocational rehabilitation program of services to blind persons. While it is true that blind persons were eligible for vocational rehabilitation services before this time, the law provided new expansion of services to all disabled individuals in such a manner as to enable the development of a sequence of services especially aimed at the handicap of blindness.

The Office of Vocational Rehabilitation, formed in 1943, became the Vocational Rehabilitation Administration twenty years later, and in 1967 became the Rehabilitation Services Administration. It has been steadily committed to an ever-increasing effort to develop methods and techniques which can enable blind persons to compete in the world of work as well as society. Public Law 565, signed into law in 1954, gave additional tools for use by Federal rehabilitation officials in the areas of personnel training and research and demonstration. Services to the blind throughout the country have benefited during the past twenty-five years from the advances which have resulted from the many efforts in short-term and long-term training programs and research and demonstration projects.

In looking back over the past thirty years, it is easy to note the tremendous progress in placing blind persons in employment situations. In fact, through the State-Federal vocational rehabilitation programs alone, the number of blind persons either entering in or returning to employment each year has had a seven-fold increase.

Today, there are nearly forty thousand identifiable occupations in the competitive field of work, and it is gratifying to note how widely blind people have fanned out into this great industrial complex.

When I first began my rehabilitation placement work, serving blind persons in the District of Columbia, I did not have the tools to work with as provided by the Barden-LaFollette Act in 1943. But employment opportunities for all persons were becoming more plentiful. The preparedness program for World War II had begun. Persons from all over were coming into the nation's Capital City to seek government employment.

In 1941 I opened the case of Bradie Adams who had come to Washington from West Virginia to seek an elevator job with the Federal government. He had sight in only one eye, and in that one he had only 10 percent of sight. That put him in the category of legal blindness. In my initial interview with him I learned that he had at one time been a machinist. I told him what other persons were doing with much less sight than what he had, but he still insisted that he was too disabled to do industrial work. I finally convinced him of his potentials, and when he found out that he would only earn $1,080 per year as an elevator operator with the government, he decided to try out for the industrial job that I had in mind for him. This changed attitude on his part was greatly helped when he discovered that I was totally blind. He thought I had perfect sight.

The following article concerning Bradie Adams appeared in the Washington *Evening Star* November 9, 1945:

DC Machinist, 90 Pct. Blind, Becomes Foreman of Shop

Although ninety percent blind, Bradie C. Adams, fifty, has become foreman of the machine shop where he began work more than four years ago as a machinist on precision work.

Mr. Adams pointed out that any blinded veteran can do the same thing if he tries. "The training and placement services offered by the Veterans Administration insure that a man can lead a useful and enjoyable life. I know this is so through my own experiences," he said.

Mr. Adams was injured during the World War when a cylinder of compressed air exploded while he was working.

He is the oldest employee in the machine shop and the third oldest employee of the company for which he works, the Flight Training Research Association. He does both supervisory and precision work.

Another interesting client I had was Edward H. Walker. I recall he came to my office with his father. He had just been graduated at the Maryland School for the Blind. In getting acquainted with him, I asked him what he had in mind so far as employment was concerned, and he told me he wanted to be a radio announcer. I had heard of a successful blind announcer somewhere in the Midwest. Since he had already been in touch with the American University, which is in the District of Columbia and where there was a course in radio announcing, I told him we would be in touch with the university and would follow through concerning his admission. His case was processed in the usual manner. A month later he was interviewed by two of the admitting officials of the university who had some doubt as to whether they could handle a blind student, but Walker told me afterwards that when they were finished with the interview, which took about an hour, they told him they would admit him.

Walker started as a student at American University in the fall of 1950. There he met Willard Scott, a second-year student, and since the two of them were interested in radio work, they started up the campus radio station. In May of 1952, Scott and Walker formed a team and put on a late show at radio station WOL. A year later when Scott became a full-time employee with radio station WRC, of the National Broadcasting Company, Walker did volunteer work at the Walter Reed Hospital on their "Bedside Network." He got

Edward H. Walker, announcer, Radio Station WWDC,
Washington, D.C.

some extra good experience in this way. At the same time he was managing the radio station at the American University on a full-time basis. He graduated from American University in 1954.

Following his graduation, Walker obtained employment at Radio Station WPGC, in Prince Georges County, a suburban area of the District of Columbia. In 1955 he was able to take on a very brief program with his friend, Willard Scott, at Radio Station WRC, which was a half-hour show called "Program Two at One." Walker facetiously referred to the title of the program as being very original since two of them were on at one o'clock. In 1956 Willard Scott went into the navy and WRC hired Walker on a full-time basis. When Scott returned from the navy, he and Walker became known as the "Joy Boys," on WRC. This two-man show lasted until October of 1972, when WRC revised its entire program. Walker and Scott then joined WWDC for two years. Willard Scott is now weather forecaster on WRC-TV and Ed Walker has just started his own show on WMAL-TV.

Walker describes the way he recently performed his duties at Radio Station WWDC, very much the same as it was with WRC. The show lasts a couple of hours a day, and Walker reads his script which he puts into braille, thus performing like any other radio station announcer, reading the ad copy in the same length of time anyone with sight would read ink print. Walker, who has been without sight all of his life, learned to read braille at a very young age. He, in describing his work, said that an engineer plays the records and does all of the technical work. While the records are being played, Walker is in contact with him by means of the intercom system, telling him what he wants to do next, and the engineer gets the next record or tape ready. Walker points at the engineer to cue him into the next sequence. Such an arrangement, Walker says, is customary in any large radio station. Thus, he is not getting any special consideration because of his blindness, as such an arrangement is carried out by radio announcers with perfect sight.

Walker meets periodically with his local advertising clients to ascertain how they like the way he is doing his job for them, which is not only good business but good public relations.

Many vocational rehabilitation counselors and placement officers have been very successful in placing blind clients on industrial jobs in almost every state. One of these persons is M. A. McCollom, employment placement consultant for the Services for the Blind and Visually Handicapped of the Kansas State Department of Social Welfare. It has been my privilege to know Mr. McCollom for the past thirty years. He has been recognized for his outstanding work in vocational rehabilitation of the blind, having received many awards. Mr. McCollom describes the unusual work being done by Steven Ceglar.

Mr. Ceglar is one of five totally blind workers placed at the John Deere Tractor Company in Waterloo, Iowa, late in 1943 by Mr. McCollom, who was at that time placement officer for the Iowa Commission for the Blind. Mr. Ceglar started on a five-spindle drill press at the rate of seventy cents an hour. During the past twenty-nine years he has worked some 150 jobs—drilling, reaming, spot facing, chamfering and tapping on a variety of castings. He developed a knowledge of various scales and gauges along with working properties of metals. His skill in handling a wide variety of jigs includes large, heavy castings as well as precision drilling on smaller parts. His skill and accuracy developed over a period of years enables him to run as high as 150 percent on many operations. Ten years ago the entire machinery was replaced due to wear.

Mr. Ceglar's most recent pay check averaged $6.64 per hour. His income for 1972 exceeded $15,000.

Prior to his loss of sight, Mr. Ceglar was a coal miner where he lost the sight of one eye at an early age from a dynamite cap. Later, as a farmer, at the age of twenty-three while

121

Steven Ceglar with the John Deere Tractor
Company, Waterloo, Iowa.

hammering on a piece of equipment, a steel chip caught him in the good eye and took the rest of his sight.

Mr. Ceglar has a wife, three children, and four grandchildren. He has remodeled the kitchen in his suburban home, and has a two-car garage, having driven every nail in the building.

Mr. McCollom also describes the work of another interesting client, Mrs. Betty Dowdy, for whom he obtained employment January 4, 1965. Mrs. Dowdy is employed in Central Service at the Kansas University Medical Center in Kansas City, Kansas. At the time of her placement, she, being totally deaf, had sufficient sight to read lips in good light. She attended the Central School for the Deaf in Saint Louis and later completed work on her Bachelor degree at Gallaudet College for the Deaf in Washington, D.C., with a major in chemistry. By this time it was known that her sight would probably be entirely gone in about ten years. It was agreed that she should be able to continue her work on a variety of operations after this occurred.

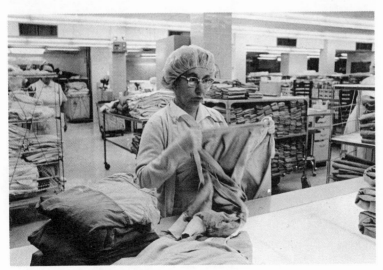

Mrs. Betty Dowdy with the Kansas University
Medical Center, Kansas City, Kansas.

Mrs. Dowdy's work varies from day to day, as she may work in a team folding laundry or work alone putting up OB packs and a variety of surgical trays or equipment packages used in preparing patients for surgery.

Mrs. Eckerberg, Mrs. Dowdy's supervisor, is most complimentary as to the quality and quantity of her performance on the job.

John Kench, employment specialist of the Grand Rapids Regional Office, Michigan Department of Social Services, sent me an interesting account of John Mulder which appeared in the Grand Rapids *Press* on June 14, 1970. Mr. Mulder became totally blind in 1957. At the time he was engaged

John Mulder in his home workshop, McBain, Michigan.

in farming on a 160-acre farm near McBain, Michigan. After one year, he sold his farm equipment and cattle and set up shop in a small building next to his home on the farm as he had always been handy with tools and working with wood. His woodworking tools consist of a table saw, miter saw, handsaws, band saw, saber saw, drill press, lathe, belt and disc sanders, drills, oscillating hand sander, power wrench and screw driver, air compressor, drum sander, grinder, and other small tools. Mulder's specialty is making picnic tables out of pine. He produces six different tables: six-foot, seven-foot, and eight-foot tables with benches attached, and six-foot, seven-foot, and eight-foot three piece sets (a table and two unattached benches). Other items that he makes include junior tables, children's tables, park benches, children's seats for picnic tables, folding chairs, stationary lawn chairs, wren, bluebird, and purple martin houses with four to twenty-four compartments, bird feeders, lawn windmills, small and large doll beds and doll cradles. "Actually," Mulder says, "I can make most anything out of wood. I feel it's easier to make a product than reading a pattern or having it read to me. All I have to do is feel it."

Mr. Kench also sent me an account of another very interesting client of his. He is Christian Vander Stel of Grand Rapids, Michigan. Mr. Vander Stel lost his sight in 1967, and after his orientation to blindness, he became employed with Steelcase, Inc., in the manufacture of office steel furniture. He started as an assembler in the "File Assembly Department." Through the courtesy of the Grand Rapids *Press,* as of January 18, 1970, the following is an account of how he performed his work.

"The job," Vander Stel said, "consists of the assembling of the inside of a filing cabinet drawer. First, there's a piece of metal they call a compressor. It's about the size of a typewritten sheet of paper, what they call letter size. The flat piece of metal has a design stamped into it, the edges are turned up and on either edge there's a slot. The bottom edge is rolled over to take away the sharpness. And in that there's about a three-inch slot.

"Into the two side slots you slide a bar about a quarter-inch wide and it extends through either side of these slots of this compressor. There's a hole on both sides just inside where the compressor would come. You slip a spring in either

Christian Vander Stel with Steelcase, Inc.,
Grand Rapids, Michigan.

hole and hook it to a little ear that sticks out on the side of this compressor.

"Then you take what I call a handle and slide it into the three-inch slot and then it stamps over and will lay on the bar that I put in previously. There are two prongs that extend beyond that and when you bring the head of the machine down, it bends these two prongs around underneath and cuts the front edge on either side and that firms the handle onto the bar. So when you set the compressor up, you have spring action with the bar." Vander Stel says he has never been involved in an industrial accident.

The Grand Rapids *Press* describes how Mr. Vander Stel learned to use the long cane for his mobility instruction with the help of a professional mobility instructor. This is the system used throughout the country, especially where there are rehabilitation centers for the adult blind.

When Mr. Vander Stel realized that his sight could not be restored, he contacted the rehabilitation counselor for the Department of Social Services. He was referred to Marvin Weessies, director of rehabilitation of the Association for the Blind and for Sight Conservation. Mr. Vander Stel described his mobility training in the following way:

"The mobility program—a very good one—is really involved and it sort of surprised me. My mobility instructor told me right away that there would be times I would be discouraged, that I would want to quit . . . with the hard work there are frustrations. I found out the second day what my mobility instructor really meant. I was just about ready to throw in the towel. I was in the association building and walking the corridors on the fourth floor with my instructor. She'd be talking and ask the direction I was going. . . . It was a problem to get my sense of direction." Learning the inside of the building was Vander Stel's first phase of his mobility instruction.

In describing the "touch technique" of the cane use, Mr. Vander Stel says, "This is where you have a long cane stretched out in front of you and as you bring your right foot forward, your cane should go to the left and touch the floor to the left. And when you step forward with your left foot the cane should come back and touch the floor to the right. And it should make an arc and shouldn't go any more than an inch on either side of your body."

Mr. Vander Stel's out-of-doors instruction took place over an area about five blocks square where there was little traffic. He said, "The first thing you have to do is learn the streets that are in this area."

In this particular area, Mr. Vander Stel said, he was told to go to a certain street. He was familiar with the area, but in trying to reach his destination, he had to take account of how many blocks he had walked, and how many turns he had made. He often became confused as to how many blocks he actually walked. It took him three weeks to master this particular area.

Vander Stel said, "One of the most difficult things for a blind person just learning is to get by open areas such as parking lots." Once, he found himself in a parking lot and called out to his instructor that he must be in such a place. All the help he got from her was the suggestion that he find his way out of it. He, after some trial and error, finally found his way out, making good use of his orientation instructions which are part of the mobility course.

Vander Stel said the key to walking on the streets is the ability to zero in on the traffic. "This was the hardest lesson I had to learn; it's a lesson you have to master. As I'm walking down the sidewalk and there are cars passing me, I always pay attention to their sounds because if I'm walking parallel with the traffic, then I know I'm going in a straight line. It's not so difficult if you are walking along and there's a line of buildings to your right, because you can follow this. You know you won't veer off, but the open spaces are the problems. A blind person doesn't walk in a straight line all the time, and when he does get off the course, he can pick up the straight line again by listening to the traffic."

Vander Stel said that when he went to the association for his rehabilitation training, he was determined he would succeed with it. This determination, he stated, is what is needed for ultimate success. When he had completed the fourteen-week program, he was able to go anywhere in Grand Rapids by himself.

Rehabilitation counselors and placement officers representing vocational rehabilitation agencies and other similar organizations dealing with the blind and the visually handicapped should keep in constant touch with the personnel offices of industrial establishments. The educating of such persons as to the abilities of the blind and visually handicapped is not a one-time job. Personnel officers go from industry to industry, and the new man or woman who took his place must be educated. This is part of the public relations responsibility and duties of every rehabilitation and placement officer.

The American Mutual Insurance Alliance in cooperation with the President's Committee on Employment of the Handicapped has published the following article entitled, "Hiring the Handicapped: Facts & Myths," which relates to all handicapped persons, but the philosophy set forth in the article is true of the blind and visually handicapped as well:

Message to Employers

Your workmen's compensation insurance carrier wholeheartedly encourages you to hire handicapped workers.

Be assured that workmen's compensation insurers do not penalize an employer for hiring disabled persons. Properly selected and placed, persons with handicaps make excellent employees. Their safety records are at least as good as those of other employees, often better.

Providing jobs for the handicapped is good business—good for them, for you, and for the American system of private enterprise.

"If we don't do something about the disabled, the chronically ill, and the older age group in our economy, by 1980 for every

129

able-bodied worker in America there will be at least one physically handicapped, one chronically ill, or one beyond the age of 65 on that worker's back."

Dr. Howard A. Rusk
Director of the Institute of Physical Medicine
and Rehabilitation, New York University
Medical Center

This nation's economic strength—our ability to grow and possibly our future as a free nation—depends on full and effective use of our manpower. While many employers are giving increased recognition to the competence of handicapped and elderly workers, there still remains a sizable reservoir of employable manpower among these groups which is not being fully utilized.

Industry is not being asked to hire these workers simply because they are handicapped, but because it is sound business practice to do so. When several million Americans who want to and could work must live as public charges, business as well as society's interests are badly served.

Unfortunately, a number of persistent myths has long militated against hiring of the handicapped. Three of the most frequently heard are:

That handicapped workers are more likely to have accidents than other employees.

That an employer's workmen's compensation insurance rates will rise if he hires handicapped workers, and

That his insurance company "won't let him" hire handicapped persons.

ALL OF THESE ARE FALSE.

U. S. Department of Labor surveys have shown that "impaired persons" have fewer disabling injuries than the average workers exposed to the same work hazards. They have about the same number of minor injuries as other workers. When placed in suitable jobs, they are for all practical purposes no longer handicapped. And since they are not inherently "unsafe," the handicapped cannot adversely affect workmen's compensation rates. These rates are based solely on the relative hazards of a company's operations and on the company's accident experience.

Insurance Position

As to insurance companies' position on such hiring, the very fact that insurers are among the leaders in rehabilitation and

130

placement of impaired workers refutes the idea that they oppose hiring the handicapped.

Property-liability insurers have repeatedly pointed out the good work records of most handicapped workers. Absenteeism among them is no greater—and is often less—than among non-handicapped workers. They are often the most loyal of workers, and their overall quit rate is about the same as for other employees. When placed in jobs they can handle, handicapped workers as a group produce at slightly higher rates than unimpaired workers on the same jobs.

Too often, however, the practice has been to consider partially disabled workers capable of only the unskilled, routine type of work. This attitude can be more crippling than the physical injury.

The trends toward automation and specialization in industry today are to the advantage of handicapped workers. A highly trained computer engineer, for example, performs his vital job perfectly well at Hughes Aircraft Company in California though he has been almost totally paralyzed by polio for five years.

(Hughes, incidentally, employs several thousand handicapped workers in jobs involving research, development and manufacture of highly specialized electronic equipment. The company has safety records and insurance savings as well as high production to attest to the value of its nondiscriminatory hiring policy.)

A large Chicago insurance company has found that deaf-mutes make better-than-average file clerks and checkers because they are able to concentrate so well, unaffected by office noise and distractions. Other deaf persons have won praise for their performance as linotype, tabulator and key-punch operators.

Blind workers, with their sense of touch often extremely highly developed to compensate for the lack of sight, have made superior assemblers, inspectors, sorters and counters of small parts in such vital industries as electronics, aircraft and missile production.

Cerebral palsy victims have been trained to use precision hand tools, and paraplegics are working very productively on assembly lines.

The use of prosthetic devices often is so skilled that once-helpless amputees can perform virtually any job they could do before their loss.

Of course, not every handicapped worker is a paragon. Persons with impairments share other human frailties common to us all.

131

But employer surveys have shown that handicapped workers often have unusually good morale and work attitudes, perhaps because they find it difficult to get work and are grateful when they are able to do so.

Personnel Suggestions

Employers who have had satisfactory experience in hiring the handicapped suggest a five-point personnel approach.

Stop thinking of impaired people as "disabled." This description was adopted to soften the word "crippled," but the connotations of "disabled" are even more painful. The word implies across-the-board inability to perform, and this is not true.

Don't dismiss the idea of employing impaired workers without finding out what they can do—on a fair and equitable basis.

Let these workers compete. Many people, in a sincere effort to help, actually make things more difficult for the handicapped. Their human and economic needs are best served when they can become self-supporting and thereby make their contribution as self-reliant members of society.

Recognize the handicapped as individuals—and deal with them that way. Sometimes their physical problems limit the scope of their activities, but they should be considered and recognized for their individual skills.

Don't patronize people with physical disabilities. The handicapped don't want to be coddled or fussed over.

One final note. There is a tendency to view the hiring of such workers as requiring of the employer some peculiar amalgam of philanthropy, altruism, and pity.

Actually, the process requires no exceptional qualifications of the employer, no special combination of time, place or circumstances. It is simply an opportunity likely to be—sooner or later—presented to every businessman. The only problem lies in being able to look beyond the applicant's disability to the basic employment question: Can the man do the job?

Hopefully, this will be recorded as one problem we shared and solved.

132

Chapter 12

Randolph-Sheppard Vendors of America

More than three thousand blind persons are currently employed in the operation of vending stands and machines in the Federal-State Randolph-Sheppard programs in the United States. As these employment opportunities have grown, so have the problems of merchandising and of competition with other interests. In recent years, blind operators of vending concessions have become increasingly aware of their mutual interests and need for an organized effort in which the operators themselves can act to protect their interests and to enlarge vending opportunities for themselves and other blind persons.

Associations of operators were formed in several states, but it was not until a group of blind operators met at the 1967 convention of the American Council of the Blind that a plan was made for a national organization of blind persons in the vending field. Plans for the organization were developed with intermediate meetings culminating in the first national convention of vendors on July 15, 1969, in Charlotte, North Carolina. This organization is the Randolph-Sheppard Vendors of America, named after the authors of the act of Congress adopted in 1936. Its five officers and eight directors are themselves blind operators of vending concessions in eleven states. Recognizing that many blind vendors do not work within the Randolph-Sheppard programs, the field of membership was broadened to include any blind person engaged

133

in vending concessions in the United States. The organization's statement of purpose is as follows:

A. Provide a forum for discussions of the views of licensed operators and blind employees affected by the Randolph-Sheppard program.
B. Protect the interest of blind persons engaged in the operation of vending stands and machines.
C. Promote the extension of the Randolph-Sheppard program.
D. Assist in promoting the purposes of the American Council of the Blind through affiliation with that organization.

A charter has been obtained in the District of Columbia for this national membership organization.

The purpose of the American Council of the Blind is to strive for the betterment of our total community: (A) Through a representative national organization primarily of blind people. (B) By providing a forum for the views of the blind from all corners of the nation and from all walks of life. (C) By elevating the social, economic and cultural level of the blind. (D) By improving educational and rehabilitational facilities. (E) By broadening vocational opportunities. (F) By encouraging and assisting the blind, especially the newly blind, to develop their abilities and potentialities and to assume their responsible places in the community. (G) By cooperating with the public and private institutions and agencies of and for the blind. (H) By providing for the free exchange of ideas, opinions and information relative to matters of concern to blind people through publication of a braille magazine. (I) By conducting a program of public education aimed toward improving the understanding of the problems of blindness and of the capabilities of blind people.

I am in receipt of a statement from E. L. Woodard, director of the Division of Employment Opportunities of the Oregon Commission for the Blind, in which he outlines the Business Enterprises program for his state. Mr. Woodard's statement is as follows:

Business Enterprises of Oregon

The Business Enterprises program in Oregon was started in November 1947 with a unit in government leased buildings in Portland, Oregon. The Administrator at that time, Mr. Clifford Stocker, took the change from his pocket and placed it in the cash drawer for the starting fund and the program was launched. From this unauspicious beginning the program grew to its present 28 units located in Federal, state and county buildings and in private industrial plants.

The Business Enterprises program of Oregon is basically oriented to snack-bar and cafeteria operations as evidenced by the fact that only 3 units of the 28 are dry vending stands (tobacco and candy products only). Oregon also has enacted legislation giving preference in food service and vending in state owned or leased buildings to the visually handicapped. This law, which we call the "Little Randolph-Sheppard," is much broader than the Randolph-Sheppard Act as it gives preference to food service as well as packaged products. This enables the operation of cafeterias and snack-bars with food being prepared upon the premises.

Prior to being assigned to the management of a unit all prospective managers are given a careful screening and training. The training is conducted in a special training unit with emphasis upon business management, food cost, public relations, sanitation, cashiering, merchandising and bookkeeping. This training is for a minimum of 6 months but may be longer if deemed necessary in specific instances.

All unit operators are united in an organization of Blind Business Managers Association (BBMA), an affiliate of the Randolph-Sheppard Vendors of America (RSVA). BBMA holds quarterly meetings in various areas of the state and also sponsors semiannual in-service training sessions. The officers of the BBMA are also members of an advisory committee for the Business Enterprises Program.

The B.E. Program is governed by the Director of Employment Opportunities Division of the Commission for the Blind. The Director is assisted in the supervision of the individual units by his Business Enterprises representatives. An advisory committee consisting of the officers of BBMA, the Director, and 3 members appointed by the Commission for the Blind, meets regularly and sets policy, goals and objectives of the program.

The enclosed photos are examples of the various unit operations of this program.

135

Steward Donaldson, operator in Multnomah County
Courthouse, Portland, Oregon.

L. E. Jeffries, operator in Medford Post Office
building, Medford, Oregon.

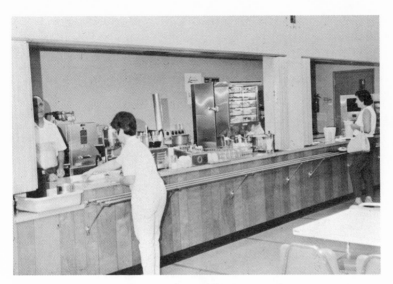

Bruce Mapes, operator of cafeteria, Crown-Zellerbach
Corporation, Portland, Oregon.

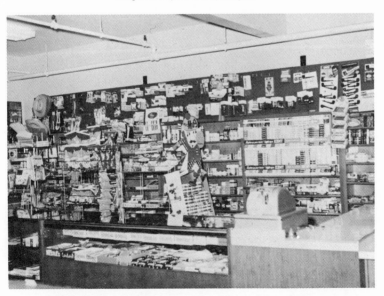

Sundry counter operated by Clay Rambo in the Fairview Hospital and
Training Center for Retarded Children, Fairview, Oregon.

137

1. Dry stand in Multnomah County Courthouse, Portland, Oregon; Steward Donaldson, blind veteran, is operator. The cigarette machine in the front of the unit is for after hours service to the building occupants. "Stew" fills and services this machine as well as 4 other candy and cigarette vendors in the areas of this building.

2. Snack-bar located in lobby of Medford Post Office Building, Medford, Oregon. L. E. "Ned" Jeffries is operator. This unit serves pastry, sandwiches, soup and hot and cold drinks as well as the other items of usual dry stand operations. A cold drink machine, cigarette and candy vendor in the Post Office "Swing Room" are serviced daily by this operator and all the profit (not a percentage from a vending company) is earned by Ned.

3. Cafeteria in Western Waxide Division of Crown-Zellerbach Corp., Portland, Oregon. Bruce Mapes is the operator. He is assisted by a sighted assistant who prepares hot lunches, soups, chili, salads, etc. Bruce makes all coffee, takes cash and washes all dishes in the automatic dishwasher in the background. Bruce also has a bank of vending machines for use of the swing and graveyard shifts.

4. This photo of sundry counter is included to show the versatility of the blind in operating all types of units. The Fairview Hospital and Training Center for Retarded Children Snack Shop is operated by Clay Rambo. He has in addition to the shown sundries, a cafeteria employing 3 assistants and innumerable "patients" as part-time dishwashers and delivery boys. This enables the snack shop to not only serve the customers but also acts as an aid to the training and correction of the retarded through work experience.

I am also in receipt of statements written by some of the vending stand operators themselves, which tell of their interests and feelings as vending stand operators. The following one is from Mrs. Grace Booker of Columbia, Tennessee:

> I received your letter requesting that I express my thoughts about the vending stand program of the rehabilitation of the blind. I think it is one of the greatest programs that the state could have established.
>
> I operate a vending stand, and to me this is not just a job. It is a feeling of independence and security. This job makes me feel as if I am the same as other people. It is not security for financial

Mrs. Grace Booker, operator, Columbia, Tennessee.

conditions alone, but security for the mind and the heart. Working in this stand has granted me the opportunity to meet new people and get new ideas.

I work in a very small place and do not make much money, but to know that you are able to do the same things that other people do means just as much to me as it would to a person who makes a million dollars.

Ever since I have been working in this stand, I have had some very nice people from the state working with me. They have never failed to help me at any time.

I lost my sight at the age of fifteen. I was going to public school at the time. I finished my education at the Tennessee School for the Blind. I took up Business Education in North Carolina and Stand Training in Memphis, Tennessee. During all this time I had only one thing on my mind. That was getting a *JOB*. Your program made it possible for my dream to be fulfilled. For this help I want to thank you all.

Another statement from a vending stand operator was received from Raymond James who is with the District of Columbia vending stand program. His statement is as follows:

The vending stand program for the blind, set up by congressional action in 1936, is truly a new way of life for those of us fortunate enough to benefit by it. For me it has meant security, self-confidence and independence. It has enabled me to become a tax-paying, self-supporting citizen instead of a burden on society.

I am most grateful to all connected with the program and may it continue its blessed work in the service of humanity.

A statement was received from Cosmo J. Liberti, of Rockville, Maryland, who is one of the vending stand operators licensed by the Department of Vocational Rehabilitation of Maryland in cooperation with the Maryland Workshop for the Blind. His statement is as follows:

Monday, May 27, 1968, was one of two days long to be remembered. I had shaved, dressed, and was having breakfast when I noticed a red tint in my vision. I drove to the school where I was a secondary school teacher of chemistry, physics, and biology. By the end of the third period, I was unable to see the students. The red tint became a deep red color. My wife was called and took me to an ophthalmologist who informed me that due to diabetes mellitus and excessive hypertension, I had had retinal hemorrhages during the night. His prognosis was dim. With my wife's assistance I was able to finish my contract year, without sight. On July 11, 1968, I was sent to Johns Hopkins Hospital Eye Clinic, where I was informed that I was totally and permanently blind.

At this time I knew the meaning of fear, despair, frustration, and panic. I had a family to support. I had three college degrees. My whole life was centered on science and science teaching. Being blind finished my entire career since no blind teachers were hired in the Maryland county where I lived. As time passed on, the panic became greater.

Unbeknowing to me my eye doctor informed the Montgomery County vocational rehabilitation officer for the blind who immediately called for an appointment to visit me the next day. He convinced me of the need for rehabilitation to overcome my handicap. I was enrolled at and attended the Columbia Lighthouse for the Blind in the District of Columbia where I was instructed in mobility and braille, and other subjects to help a blind person.

My vocational rehabilitation counselor attempted to place me

140

in teaching. I instructed at several schools for a two-week period at each place. I was evaluated at these schools by principals and assistant principals and the assistant superintendent without my knowledge. At the conclusion of each day I was congratulated by those concerned on my knowledge of science and my teaching

Raymond James, operator, Treasury Department
building, Washington, D.C.

141

Cosmo J. Liberti, operator, Health, Education,
and Welfare building, Rockville, Maryland.

ability. However, the county superintendent would not approve any contract because I would, in their opinion, be unable to handle my disciplinary problems.

My teaching career was really over. The favorable teaching evaluations were of no avail. Three degrees meant nothing. The panic grew greater.

Then I was told about the vending stand program for the blind by my vocational rehabilitation counselor. I was interviewed by the director of the Maryland Workshop for the Blind and offered the opportunity to become a trainee with the objective of managing a vending stand upon the successful completion of my training program. I readily accepted the challenge because it offered me the great opportunity to prove myself as to my ability to work with other people.

I have now demonstrated my ability as a vending stand operator, and I am very happy with my new work.

Senator Jennings Randolph was very elated by the formation of the Randolph-Sheppard Vendors of America, and he

142

made this clear in a letter he wrote to John Thomas, its first president. The letter reads as follows:

July 11, 1969

Mr. John Thomas, President
Randolph-Sheppard Vendors of America
The White House Inn
Charlotte, North Carolina

Dear Mr. Thomas:

I am very pleased to learn of the formation of your organization and flattered that its name is taken from legislation I helped to write 33 years ago.

The first convention of the Randolph-Sheppard Vendors of America on July 15 is a very noteworthy occasion, and I wish the new association every success. It is by joining together in such groups that people with common interests and concerns can make themselves heard.

I have been proud of my part in the Randolph-Sheppard Act ever since it was passed in 1936, not because of any personal accomplishment but because this legislation opened the door of pride and achievement to so many people. From its modest beginning, the vending stand program has experienced a steady growth until today there are nearly 3,300 blind people involved in its operations.

In addition to providing employment, this program has helped to break down the barriers that once existed to prevent handicapped people from participating fully in our society. The demonstrations of ability by the blind facilitated the acceptance of all types of handicapped workers by industry and influenced the establishment of public policy to provide training and job opportunities for handicapped citizens.

I have kept abreast of developments in this area and on June 20 introduced a bill to bring the Randolph-Sheppard Act into line with contemporary conditions and requirements. This is the first time in 15 years that changes to the act have been proposed, and I believe they will make the program even more valuable than it has been in the past.

Once again, my congratulations to the new association and to you as its first president.

Very truly,
JENNINGS RANDOLPH

Chapter 13

Economics of the Randolph-Sheppard Program

Every year the Department of Health, Education, and Welfare sends to the state licensing agencies under the Randolph-Sheppard Act what is known as an Information Memorandum which reports on the vending stand program for the preceding fiscal governmental year, both from a national point of view as well as an analysis by states.

Quoting from the Information Memorandum for the fiscal year ending June 30, 1972:

> The most significant achievement in the national program was the increase in gross sales to $109,800,000. This represents an 8.4 percent gain over the previous year. Net proceeds to operators advanced to $22,800,000 reflecting a 10.5 percent gain, returning an annual average income of $6,996 to 3,583 blind operators.

According to the Information Memorandum, the total number of all stands was 3,229. The total gross sales in actual dollars was $109,847,028. The total number of operators was 3,583. Net proceeds to operators in actual dollar figures was $22,768,349. The total number of stands in Federal buildings was 878; in non-Federal locations, 2,351, of which 1,436 were public and 915 were private. The total gross sales in the Federal locations amounted to $32,213,449; in non-Federal locations, $77,633,579. Total number of operators in Federal locations was 1,005; in non-Federal locations, 2,578. The net proceeds to the operators in Federal locations amounted to $6,610,786; in non-Federal locations, $16,157,563.

144

From the above figures which show 878 Federal locations, it is obvious that the Randolph-Sheppard Act paved the way to thousands of additional vending stand opportunities for blind persons in the non-Federal locations. It is estimated that there are at least two hundred additional Federal locations that are available for the program and many thousands of non-Federal locations which the licensing agencies can obtain. At the present time Senator Randolph is sponsoring Federal legislation as amendments to the Randolph-Sheppard Act which will greatly increase the vending stand opportunities for blind persons. The information contained in the preceding chapter of this book makes it clear that the vending stand program is a practical and logical project for the vocational rehabilitation of blind persons.

Were it not for the Randolph-Sheppard vending stand program, it is conservatively estimated that one-half of the present vending stand operators would be on public assistance. As single individuals, their average annual income from this source would amount to $1,500. This means that the total annual outlay of Federal and state funds would amount to $2,686,500. The average annual income for the same number of persons—1,791—as married individuals and as heads of families would amount to $3,000, or an annual outlay of welfare funds amounting to $5,373,000.

The following table is the accumulative vending stand program statistics from 1952 to 1972, inclusive, showing by the Federal government fiscal year the average net earnings of operators, number of operators, number of vending stands, and total gross sales.

In the twenty-one-year period from 1952 to 1972, inclusive, the total gross sales amounted to $1,101,939,757.

Vending Stand Program Statistics (1952-1972)

Fiscal Year	Average Net Earnings of Operators	Number of Operators	Number of Vending Stands	Total Gross Sales
1952	$1,956	1,513	1,479	$ 18.7M
1953	2,209	1,581	1,543	20.6M
1954	2,193	1,659	1,599	22.0M
1955	2,345	1,721	1,664	23.5M
1956	2,532	1,804	1,727	25.8M
1957	2,654	1,924	1,830	28.9M
1958	2,833	1,998	1,901	31.7M
1959	3,354	2,111	1,982	34.8M
1960	3,688	2,216	2,078	38.2M
1961	3,900	2,332	2,174	42.0M
1962	4,140	2,425	2,257	45.7M
1963	4,392	2,542	2,365	49.5M
1964	4,452	2,641	2,442	53.9M
1965	4,716	2,806	2,574	59.4M
1966	4,932	2,915	2,661	65.3M
1967	5,244	3,117	2,807	71.5M
1968	5,580	3,259	2,918	79.0M
1969	5,868	3,341	3,002	86.4M
1970	6,300	3,352	3,061	93.9M
1971	6,540	3,454	3,142	101.3M
1972	6,996	3,583	3,229	109.8M

The following statement concerning the vending stand program was received from Robert R. Nathan, a nationally well-known economist:

> In our free enterprise society it is of utmost importance that individuals achieve independence and self-respect through producing goods and services and supporting themselves. Of course there are some who cannot possibly be self-supporting and who need public assistance but whenever and wherever handicapped individuals are assisted in some way or other to become contributors to our economy and thereby achieve economic independence it is a wonderful accomplishment.
>
> Over the years not only have countless numbers of blind people benefitted but I think this has helped the country. I note that gross sales of the activities under the Randolph-Sheppard Act

146

as conducted by the blind increased from $18 million in January 1952 to nearly $110 million in fiscal 1972. That is a remarkable growth and the latter figure is by no means economically insignificant. Nor is the accumulative total over the years minor. It is truly impressive that in 21 years sales from these retail stands run by blind persons, have aggregated over $1.1 billion.

Again, I would emphasize that this is not only an important factor for the individuals involved but also for the economy and there it is an indirect benefit as well as a direct benefit. I say that because it encourages other disadvantaged persons in their pursuit of economic independence. Providing jobs for thousands of people and providing added services for millions of customers is truly a creative and constructive economic as well as human venture.

Chapter 14

Awards and Retirement

After thirty-three years I retired from government service effective at the close of business on March 31, 1971. My work was very enjoyable as I was always promoting some government project or cause in connection with work as a vocational rehabilitation supervisor. Carrying a caseload in the early years and working closely with the rehabilitation counselors on my staff in the later years, I was either directly or indirectly involved with the success of each client's rehabilitation. It was always gratifying and pleasurable when closing a case as rehabilitated to spell out in detail the successful work the client was engaged in and the steps leading to that successful placement. I am sure this is the feeling of all rehabilitation counselors when they succeed with the placement and rehabilitation of their visually impaired clients.

From the standpoint of the visually impaired client himself, his cause is always served best if he seeks the assistance and counseling of a vocational rehabilitation office at the earliest date possible after it has been determined by his ophthalmologist that his vision will be permanently impaired. If he delays doing this, he can become despondent, and thus make it more difficult for him to respond to good professional advice.

During the lifetime of anyone in public office, it is not unlikely that he or she will have received an award in recognition of services well done. This was my pleasure on many occasions, but I would like to tell about four of them as they meant so much to me.

On July 18, 1970, I was awarded the Ambassador Award of the American Council of the Blind, at the annual convention banquet of the council in Oklahoma City. The Award, in part, reads as follows:

> In recognition of outstanding performance as a citizen of his community, state and nation. By his example of a full, active life, dedicated to the public interest, he has rendered invaluable service to the total blind community by improving the public's understanding of the abilities and potentialities of blind persons. He is therefore considered worthy to be designated as AMBASSADOR EXTRAORDINARY OF THE BLIND.

I received another award at this convention which was given to me by the Randolph-Sheppard Vendors of America, which organization was holding its second annual convention in Oklahoma City in conjunction with the American Council of the Blind. At their Tuesday luncheon, July 14, 1970, both Senator Randolph and I were their guests. Each of us received a very heavy plaque, appropriately worded, which was presented to us by the president. The bronze plaque is mounted on a beautiful wooden base, and I recall Senator Randolph saying that he had received many awards and plaques, but this one was the heaviest.

The third award I am very fond of, and which was given to me in 1970, is known as the Leo Axlrod Memorial Award. Mr. Axlrod, for many years, was chairman of the Employment of the Handicapped Committee of B'nai B'rith District Five. The award is given each year by Mrs. Libbie Axlrod in the memory of her husband, to honor some man or woman, who is a member of B'nai B'rith, and who has helped to create equal employment opportunities for the handicapped in every area wherein a B'nai B'rith lodge and chapter is located. The award is in the form of a beautiful rattan chair which is manufactured in the Axlrod owned factory, the Empire Furniture and Rattan Works, where only physically

149

handicapped persons are employed. This factory is in the area of Coral Gables, Florida.

The fourth award of which I am very proud is a Presidential Citation given me by William P. McCahill on April 2, 1971, on the occasion of my retirement luncheon. Mr. Mc-Cahill was executive secretary of the President's Committee on Employment of the Handicapped. This committee is responsible for, and works in close cooperation with, the Governor's Committee on Employment of the Handicapped in every state. It has done a tremendous job in public relations for the betterment of all handicapped persons through its splendid efforts in bringing about a better understanding on the part of employers of the capabilities of the handicapped.

This retirement luncheon, which took place on Friday, April 2, 1971, and which was presided over by Edward H. Walker, of radio fame, was arranged by one of my former secretaries, Mrs. Thelma Ross. I became aware of her efforts after she had gotten along with the arrangements up to a certain point, and it was then that she told me what she was up to and asked me for a list of persons to be invited. It took place in a downtown hotel, and some 250 persons turned out. This was a most enjoyable occasion, and one which I shall never forget.

On this occasion my chief, Norman W. Pierson, read me the letter which his department had prepared, and one which I shall always cherish. Mr. Pierson was a very capable director, and under his leadership the department's services to the handicapped had tripled in scope. His letter reads as follows:

> Not often do I have the privilege of writing an employee of our Vocational Rehabilitation Administration on the occasion of a well-earned retirement after 33 years of devoted public service. It is a great pleasure for me to send this letter in recognition, as well as appreciation, of the innovative and exceptional contributions you have made toward improvement of services for both The Nation and The District's handicapped.
>
> Not only have you pioneered in the field of rehabilitation—

William P. McCahill, right, presenting a Presidential Citation to Leonard A. Robinson at retirement luncheon.

Norman W. Pierson, left, and Leonard A. Robinson
at retirement luncheon for Mr. Robinson.

through your work which led to the enactment of the Randolph-Sheppard Vending Stand Program for the Blind—but also, through your concern and dedication in serving the District's visually impaired for nearly twenty-five years. Your enthusiasm for the Vocational Rehabilitation Administration, your faithfulness in aiding its causes and your commitment in serving disabled persons on an individual basis are a happy combination of qualities which we shall surely miss.

As you depart the active arena of government service, and on behalf of your colleagues who hold you in such high esteem, may I extend our warmest wishes for continued years of happiness and fulfillment.

I shall always cherish, too, the invocation delivered by Rabbi Henry Segal of the B'nai Israel Congregation. It reads as follows:

Almighty God and Father:
One of Thy greatly gifted children, Helen Keller, bereft of the faculties of sight, speech or hearing, but yet not truly handicapped, once expressed her own assessment of her condition poetically thus:

> They took away what should have been my eyes
> But I remembered Milton's Paradise
> They took away what should have been my ears
> Beethoven came and wiped away my tears
> They took away what should have been my tongue
> But I talked with God when I was young
> He would not let them take away my soul,
> Possessing that, I still possess the whole.

Today we are assembled here to honor one of Thy greatly gifted but sightless sons, Leonard Robinson, who possessing a great soul has demonstrated that he has possessed the whole of his being, as if without any impairment whatsoever.

Possessing a great soul, he dedicated himself to making whole the lives of other handicapped sightless people, and performed humanitarian service of a rare kind and a high quality as a veritable co-worker with Thee for good among Thy children.

Long ago, the Jewish Sages taught that whoever merits to be honored and is honored among men, it is a sure sign that he is also well regarded by Thee. Leonard Robinson has richly merited the honor bestowed upon him by his fellowmen and the high esteem in which he is held by all who know him. We know that he finds great favor in Thine eyes, and we pray that Thou bless him and his loved ones with the rich rewards Thou hast vouchsafed unto all who work with Thee for good in this world.

Grant him many more good years blessed with good health, and ample opportunity to enjoy his well-earned leisure now that he has retired from active service in the important post he has held with so much credit. May he have the added joy of beholding the great work he has thus far so nobly advanced, go forward and prosper by the labors of other dedicated men and women.

For these and for Thy benign blessing and guidance do we pray Thee, and in thankfulness to Thee for Thy bounty of which we shall soon partake, we reverently say *Amen.*

To retire from active participation in my community and forget about the unfulfilled needs of the visually handicapped was never my intention. A few months before my government employment came to an end, I activated the Foundation for the Handicapped and Elderly, Inc., a nonprofit organization incorporated under the laws of the District of Columbia. Its officers agreed that what was needed most in the community at that particular time was a low-vision clinic. I assumed the presidency of the organization as a volunteer worker and set out to accomplish its immediate goal.

In almost every large city in the United States there is a low-vision clinic. Their accomplishments and availability are not generally known outside the circles of agencies for the blind. They are affiliated with agencies for the blind and with the ophthalmological departments of hospitals. The most famous hospital affiliation is the Low-Vision Clinic at the Wilmer Eye Institute of Johns Hopkins Hospital in Baltimore, under the able direction of Dr. Louise Sloan. It can be said that these clinics take over where ordinary lenses cannot improve the eyesight of certain low-vision cases. During the past twenty years, low-vision aids have been devised by outstanding members in the field of optometry and research workers working with government grants. Many of these aids have built-in lights which are helpful in some cases. The average person would describe some of these aids as super-deluxe magnifiers. There are hundreds of variations of these aids, some fitting over regular eyeglasses, and all of them prescribed by a trained technician who is either an ophthalmologist or an optometrist.

In my work as a vocational rehabilitation counselor and supervisor, I sent many of my clients to Dr. Sloan in Baltimore whom she was able to help very much. In some cases this low-vision clinic help enabled them to obtain employment in the field of their choice because they were fitted with an optical aid which gave them more useful sight, which ordinary glasses could not do. In some cases such aid enabled these clients to maintain their employment when it was believed by their personnel officers that their sight was insufficient to perform the duties of their employment. The most famous case I can recall in this category was a Federal government officer who had been in government work for over twenty years, but whose eyesight had deteriorated to the point where he felt he could no longer carry on with his important government functions. His annual salary was thirty thousand dollars. His personnel director agreed with him, but recommended that he visit the Vocational Rehabilitation Department of the district government. This occurred about eighteen months before my government retirement. His case was processed in the usual manner, and after studying his eye report which we obtained from his ophthalmologist, we decided to send him to see Dr. Sloan. She was able to furnish him with seven different optical aids which improved his sight for various kinds of reading, thus enabling him to forget about retirement with disability. With these optical aids he was promoted to a much more responsible position and he is still doing his work very well.

The success of the case just cited gave me the determination to help establish a competent low-vision clinic in my immediate community, which resulted in the action taken by the Foundation for the Handicapped and Elderly, Inc. I was particularly anxious to have this low-vision clinic in a hospital medical center, as in the case of the one at the Wilmer Eye Institute. Here, ophthalmologists working in such a medical center could have easy access to the low-vision clinic if they felt that their patients could be benefited there. Also, the good work of a low-vision clinic can be more readily brought to the attention of these physicians.

The George Washington University Medical Center in the District of Columbia was about to appoint a new director, and I was told to get in touch with Dr. Mansour Armaly in Iowa City who would be that new director. I explained to him on the telephone what I had in mind and the great need for it, and he agreed to arrange a conference with me when he came to town. I had heard a great deal of his background and successful research work in eye diseases, especially in glaucoma, and since George Washington University Hospital was a teaching hospital and vitally interested in rehabilitation work, I was very excited about the possibility of the formation of a low-vision clinic at this medical center.

I had the conference with Dr. Armaly several weeks after I first spoke to him, and he agreed to establish the low-vision clinic if I could come up with a substantial amount of money to help defray its expenses for the first two years. I told him about the foundation, and that we would raise whatever money the low-vision clinic would need. I also told him of the help I was getting from Dr. Louise Sloan who agreed with me that we should have our own low-vision clinic, and how excited she was about its possible location at the George Washington University Medical Center. Dr. Armaly had heard of her good work and he was pleased that we would have her interest and cooperation.

What we now needed was a trained technician who could take over the duties of the low-vision clinic and who would be under the direction of Dr. Armaly. I contacted Dr. Sloan and she came up with Dr. Roberto Sunga, from Manila, whom she had trained some two years back. Dr. Sunga, an ophthalmologist, had come to the Wilmer Eye Institute for additional research and there learned about the good work Dr. Sloan was doing. He became thoroughly acquainted with all of the details of such a clinic during the two years he was at the Wilmer Eye Institute and returned to Manila in the Philippines to establish such a clinic there. But this he was never able to do. Dr. Sloan wrote him at our suggestion and he was very much interested in coming here to take over the new low-vision clinic. After several months he obtained his visa and he and Mrs. Sunga arrived in July 1971.

Now, almost four years later, Dr. Sunga and Dr. Armaly can proudly boast of the good work their low-vision clinic is doing. And the foundation can proudly boast of having fulfilled its obligations. In this respect, I must give credit to the Amity Club of Washington, the Washington Society for the Blind, and the District of Columbia Association of Workers for the Blind, which organizations came forth with the necessary funds, along with certain private contributions, to join the foundation in successfully establishing this most worthy eye clinic.

I spoke before the Chillum Lions Club in Prince Georges County, Maryland, and suggested that they join the foundation and sponsor the low-vision clinic examination of the eyes of the visually impaired school children in the Prince Georges County special educational classes. They liked this idea and came forth with a substantial amount of money to accomplish the task. Many of these children have been fitted with certain optical aids which will greatly facilitate their school work which, for the most part, was previously done in braille. Thus, another dimension is added to their learning process.

When an adult or child today experiences an eye ailment which leads to greatly impaired vision, there is something available and some place to go which will ameliorate this circumstance. Advanced methods in orientation to blindness and a public better informed as to the capabilities of the visually impaired have brought the light at the tunnel end

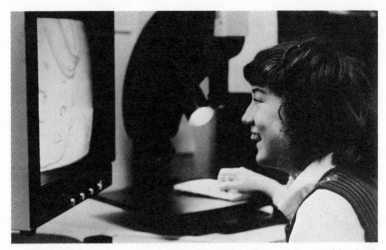

Colleen Hurley, a low-vision student from Prince Georges County, Maryland, uses a closed-circuit television reader, which magnifies printed material, at the Low Vision Clinic of the George Washington University Medical Center.

Catharine Bunnell, one of Prince Georges County's low-vision students, tries out an optical aid under the supervision of Dr. Roberto Sunga at the Low Vision Clinic of the George Washington University Medical Center, with two members of the Chillum Lions Club observing.

much closer and in full view. We must also never forget the important part that a generous Congress has played in all of this success. Much more remains to be done, however, but no wiser investment of the taxpayer's dollar can be found than in the rehabilitation of human lives.

In whatever endeavor the handicapped person finds himself, he is out to prove that ability, not disability, is what counts.

Vending Stand Report, 1973

DEPARTMENT OF HEALTH, EDUCATION, AND WELFARE
SOCIAL AND REHABILITATION SERVICE
WASHINGTON, D.C. 20201

INFORMATION MEMORANDUM

January 29, 1974
RSA-IM-74-41

TO   :   State Rehabilitation Agencies (General)
                 State Rehabilitation Agencies (Blind)

SUBJECT : Vending Stand Report for Fiscal Year 1973

CONTENT: The information contained in the attached tables has
                 been obtained and tabulated from the State agencies'
                 annual Vending Stand Reports.

A review of the data shows a continuing growth in the
vending stand program for the past fiscal year. During
FY 1973, however, a slight lag was noted in certain of
the following areas, in comparison to the previous year:
Number of stands, a 2.4 percent increase; number of
operators, 1.5 percent increase; and net proceeds to operators, 9.2 percent increase. Also noted was a continued
decline for the second year of the number of vending
stands located in Federal buildings where four less stands
were reported. Total gross sales, with 8.7 percent increase in F.Y. 1973, is slightly higher than the increase
reported for F.Y. 1972.

The information contained in the attached tables is as
follows:

Table A—National statistics comparing the program activities of F.Y. 1973 with F.Y. 1972, showing percentages of increase or decrease.

Table B—State and Regional tabulation on number of stands with percentage of increase, number of operators, and average operator earnings.

Table C—Statistical data for each State showing number of stands per 100,000 population, average annual income per operators and national ranking, set-aside funds collected less minimum return.

Table D—Provides information regarding the number of stands, population, and stands per 100,000 population in each Region.

Although not shown in tabular form, we believe the following information would be helpful to you to illustrate the growth picture over a five year period.

The number of operators increased from 3,341 in F.Y. 1969 to 3,636 in F.Y. 1973. This represents an 8.8 percent increase over the five year period. During the same time, the number of stands increased from 3,002 in F.Y. 69 to 3,307 in 1973, a 10.2 percent increase.

The average annual income per operator was $5,868 in F.Y. 69, increasing to $7,428 in F.Y. 1973, (a 26.6 percent increase).

The intent of the new vocational rehabilitation legislation is to provide rehabilitation services to a larger number of the more severely disabled. Expanding the Randolph-Sheppard vending stand program is one excellent way of achieving this goal. In line with the foregoing, we would like to make the following suggestions which the States may wish to consider:

1) Establishing realistic, substantial goals for increasing the number of vending stands and operators,

162

2) Conducting State-wide surveys to find additional feasible locations for new vending stands,

3) Mounting a concentrated effort to locate and train blind individuals having the desire and potential to become vending stand operators,

4) In the overall scheme for achieving the total VR program objectives, assign a higher priority to the vending stand program, and

5) Evaluating the vending stand program in order to update and expand areas where necessary.

We are pleased with the continued progress indicated by this report and will cooperate with you in any way possible to expand the program to its maximum potential in the coming years.

William M. Eshelman
Acting Commissioner
Rehabilitation Services
Administration

Attachments

National Summary of Statistical Data
Derived from the State's Annual Vending Stand
Reports For FY 1972 and FY 1973

	FY 1972	*FY 1973*	*Percentage Increase Over Previous Year*
Total Number All Stands	3,229	3,307	2.4
Federal Locations	878	874	−.5
Non-Federal Locations	2,351	2,433	3.5
A. Public	1,436	1,504	4.7
B. Private	915	929	1.5
Total Gross Sales	$109,847,028	$119,350,995	8.7
Federal Locations	32,213,449	33,157,731	2.9
Non-Federal Locations	77,633,579	86,193,264	11.0
Total Number of Operators	3,583	3,636	1.5
Federal Locations	1,005	1,001	−.4
Non-Federal Locations	2,578	2,635	2.2
Net Proceeds to Operators	$ 22,768,349	$ 24,856,579	9.2
Federal Locations	6,610,786	6,895,212	4.3
Non-Federal Locations	16,157,563	17,961,367	11.2
Annual Average			
Earnings of Operators	$ 6,996	$ 7,428	6.2

TABLE B
Selected Data
Annual Vending Stand Report FY 1973

Region and State	Total No. of Stands	Increase or Decrease from Stands Reported as of June 30, 1972	Total No. of Blind Operators	Annual Average Earnings of Operators
National Total	3,307	78	3,636	$7,428
I Conn.	27	-2	32	6,324
Me.	9	1	9	9,048
Mass.	37	-3	40	9,804
N.H.	8	3	8	6,492
R.I.	24	1	17	6,156
Vt.	5	-1	5	5,016
Total	110	-1	111	
II N.J.	56	-1	58	10,752
N.Y.	142	3	172	6,288
P.R.	1	–	2	4,494
Total	199	2	232	
III Del.	21	–	23	6,096
D.C.	73	-2	84	9,960
Md.	84	6	77	12,084
Penn.	191	-3	191	7,020
Va.	69	–	82	11,652
W. Va.	25	-1	36	5,064
Total	463	–	493	
IV Ala.	156	–	156	4,404
Fla.	132	7	155	8,916
Ga.	146	4	181	6,876
Ky.	54	5	78	7,608
Miss.	84	-6	74	5,196
N. Car.	110	-3	130	5,832
S. Car.	58	7	60	6,180
Tenn.	142	-1	152	5,820
Total	882	13	986	

TABLE B—*Continued*

V	Ill.	100	13	100	8,976
	Ind.	35	−2	36	4,932
	Mich.	85	9	90	6,192
	Minn.	66	2	70	8,352
	Ohio	187	5	201	7,836
	Wisc.	22	−	27	8,364
	Total	495	27	524	
VI	Ark.	94	2	98	7,092
	La.	95	−2	112	9,060
	N. Mex.	33	−2	43	7,560
	Okla.	74	1	112	4,692
	Tex.	174	14	200	7,092
	Total	470	13	565	
VII	Iowa	29	3	29	7,596
	Kans.	31	2	37	8,028
	Mo.	64	−	70	7,764
	Nebr.	19	2	16	5,100
	Total	143	7	152	
VIII	Colo.	51	3	51	9,228
	Mont.	9	−1	9	2,304
	N. Dak.	2	−	2	5,760
	S. Dak.	8	2	8	3,408
	Utah	16	−	29	4,068
	Wyo.	10	1	11	6,720
	Total	96	5	110	
IX	Ariz.	24	−	24	9,708
	Calif.	306	10	315	8,664
	Guam	2	−	2	5,784
	Hawaii	27	1	27	6,792
	Nev.	13	−	13	7,740
	Total	372	11	381	
X	Alaska	2	−	2	6,216
	Idaho	7	1	7	5,520
	Ore.	28	−	33	6,864
	Wash.	40	−	40	8,160
	Total	77	1	82	

TABLE C

Selected Comparative Data on State Vending Stand Programs

State	Vending Stands Per 100,000 Population[1]			Average Net Proceeds to Operators			Set Aside Less Minimum Return	Management Positions[2]
	No. FY 1973	Rank FY 1972	Rank FY 1973	Amount FY 1973	Rank FY 1972	Rank FY 1973	Amount	Number
National Average	1.57			$7,428			2,419,355	
Alabama	4.44	3	3	4,404	50	49	26,304	6.8
Alaska	.62	46	49	6,216*	46	32	987	—
Arizona	1.23	31	34	9,708	4	6	13,621	3
Arkansas	4.75	2	2	7,092	23	23	94,408	15
California	1.50	26	25	8,664	10	12	360,586	32.3
Colorado	2.16	17	17	9,228	6	7	73,995	7.2
Connecticut	.88	35	43	6,324	28	30	———	1
Delaware	3.72	5	4	6,096	41	36	43,782	7
Dist. of Columbia	9.76	1	1	9,960	5	4	339,099	11
Florida	1.82	20	20	8,916	13	11	138,055	16
Georgia	3.09	9	9	6,876	30	25	117,129	12
Guam	2.35	15	15	5,784	3	39	947	2
Hawaii	3.34	8	7	6,792	24	27	———	2.8

TABLE C—*Continued*

Idaho	.93	39	41	5,520	43	41	——	1
Illinois	.89	41	42	8,976	9	10	48,172	17
Indiana	.66	43	47	4,932	47	46	——	3
Iowa	1.01	36	39	7,596	36	21	——	3
Kansas	1.37	32	30	8,028	25	16	36,236	5.3
Kentucky	1.64	24	23	7,608	21	20	54,161	19
Louisiana	2.55	12	12	9,060	14	8	——	7.3
Maine	.87	40	44	9,048	12	9	3,136	.8
Maryland	2.07	18	19	12,084	1	1	251,649	10
Massachusetts	.64	44	48	9,804	7	5	——	7
Michigan	.94	38	40	6,192	31	33	58,223	——
Minnesota	1.69	22	22	8,352	19	14	62,809	7
Mississippi	3.71	4	5	5,196	45	42	80,846	12
Missouri	1.35	29	31	7,764	16	18	40,716	5
Montana	1.25	27	33	2,304	53	52	706	——
Nebraska	1.25	34	33	5,100	34	43	19,352	4
Nevada	2.47	13	14	7,740	15	19	7,694	1
New Hampshire	1.04	45	38	6,492	17	29	71	1.2
New Jersey	.76	41	46	10,752	8	3	——	6.3
New Mexico	3.10	7	8	7,560	32	22	7,853	2
New York	.77	42	45	6,288	29	31	103,072	18.7
North Carolina	2.11	16	18	5,832	33	37	——	22
North Dakota	.32	48	51	5,760	42	40	——	——

TABLE C—*Continued*

Ohio	1.73	21	21	7,836	22	17	222,761	21
Oklahoma	2.81	10	11	4,692	48	47	45,911	7.2
Oregon	1.28	31	32	6,864	27	26	17,860	2.8
Pennsylvania	1.60	23	24	7,020	20	24	212,876	20
Puerto Rico	.04	49	52	4,494	49	48	1,247	1
Rhode Island	2.48	14	13	6,156	38	35	13,011	5.2
South Carolina	2.18	19	16	6,180	44	34	——	11
South Dakota	1.18	37	35	3,408	52	51	——	1.5
Tennessee	3.52	6	6	5,820	37	38	67,058	17
Texas	1.49	28	26	7,092	26	23	137,937	14
Utah	1.42	26	28	4,068	35	50	9,649	—
Vermont	1.08	30	37	5,016	40	45	300	5
Virginia	1.45	26	27	11,652	2	2	72,251	13
Washington	1.16	33	36	8,160	11	15	——	2.5
West Virginia	1.40	25	29	5,064	51	44	10,552	8
Wisconsin	.49	47	50	8,364	18	13	16,890	2
Wyoming	2.90	11	10	6,720	39	28	3,399	2

[1] Based on population as of 7/1/72 as per Commerce Release Series P-25, No. 500, dated May 1973.

[2] These management positions are as reported by each State agency; however, some agencies include only day-to-day management personnel while others include fiscal or clerical staff.

169

TABLE D
Number of Vending Stands per 100,000 Population
by Region for Fiscal Year 1973

Region	Number of Stands	Population	Number of Stands per 100,000
I	110	12,099,000	.91
II	199	28,445,000	.70
III	463	23,840,000	1.94
IV	882	32,961,000	2.68
V	495	44,823,000	1.10
VI	470	21,046,000	2.23
VII	143	11,419,000	1.25
VIII	96	5,858,000	1.64
IX	372	23,834,000	1.56
X	77	6,706,000	1.15
National	3,307	211,031,000	1.57

Randolph-Sheppard Act

Statement by Senator Jennings Randolph (D—W.Va.) on the Need for Amendments to the 1936 Blind Vendor Act

On December 7, 1974, the President at long last signed into law H.R. 17503, the Rehabilitation Act Amendments of 1974. That measure, which is now Public Law 93-516, contains as Title II, the Randolph-Sheppard Act Amendments of 1974.

More than thirty-eight years have passed since the enactment of the first blind vendor legislation on June 20, 1936, which, with the invaluable help of the author of this book, Leonard Robinson, I sponsored in the House of Representatives.

Although the blind vendor program has been a success in terms of providing jobs and income to blind entrepreneurs, that success has been marred by a number of serious problems. Competition from automatic vending machines has increasingly threatened to suffocate the program. Employee welfare and recreation groups have refused to part with this income, even though their right to any of it is of questionable legality. The General Services Administration proposed regulations the effect of which would have been to reduce the kinds of articles to be sold by vendors in buildings it controls. That same agency has determined that its cafeteria operations have priority over the welfare of blind vendors.

Commanders of military installations have been particularly insensitive to the blind vendor program. It is even reported that an employee association at a major space installation demanded that blind vendors there give a portion of their income to the association—precisely the reverse of the spirit of the Federal law. Employees at a western Federal building boycotted and threatened a blind vendor because he was required to raise some prices slightly due to inflation.

These are but some of the obstacles encountered by blind vendors in their efforts to provide a subsistence income for their families. Other problems can be ascertained by the reader who understands the kinds of improvements made by the 1974 amendments to the Randolph-Sheppard Act. The major changes are outlined below.

First, blind vendors, for the first time, will have at their disposal a number of new administrative and judicial remedies to insure that they are fairly and properly treated through the program. State licensing agencies must provide a hearing to an aggrieved blind licensee. Vendors may also have their grievances arbitrated by an impartial panel at the Federal level. In addition, blind vendors are given standing to sue in Federal Court.

Second, a new formula requires the assignment of from 30 percent to 100 percent of vending machine income on Federal property to blind vendors and/or State licensing agencies for benefit of vendors, with certain exceptions.

Third, blind vendors are to have a priority in operating vending facilities, not just a preference.

Fourth, every new or renovated Federal or Federal agency-occupied building will, after January 1, 1975, be required to have one or more sites for blind vending facilities.

Fifth, a stronger and larger Federal office for the Blind and Visually Handicapped is mandated, to provide uniform regulations to be adopted by each State licensing agency with respect to accounting procedures, policies on selection and establishment of new vending facilities, distribution of income to blind vendors, and use and control of set-aside funds.

Sixth, the Department of Health, Education, and Welfare is to be the primary authority for the blind vendor program, and every Federal agency must adhere to HEW regulations governing the program.

Seventh, set-aside funds may be used for retirement, health insurance payments, and paid sick leave and vacation time for blind vendors. Vending machine income accruable to State agencies must first be used for these purposes.

Eighth, additional job training, upward mobility, and follow-along services must be provided to blind licensees.

Ninth, each State agency must give blind licensees access to financial data on the program and help develop and sustain a Committee of Blind Vendors in each State, which will participate in major program and policy decisions of each agency which affect the program.

Finally, a number of other changes have been made which are designed to broadly benefit the blind vendor program. A one-year residency requirement for blind vendors is eliminated, as is the requirement that a vendor be twenty-one years of age. Cafeterias are added as vending facilities, and the kinds of merchandise which may be sold are greatly expanded.

Following this statement are the findings regarding the operation of the blind vending stand program enacted as part of Title II of Public Law 93-516, Ninety-third Congress, H.R. 17503, December 7, 1974; and a reprinting of the Randolph-Sheppard Act, incorporating the Amendments of 1974 as specified in P.L. 93-516.

Jennings Randolph, Chairman
Subcommittee on the Handicapped
United States Senate
Washington, D. C.
December 20, 1974

Findings

SEC. 201. The Congress finds—

(1) after review of the operation of the blind vending stand program authorized under the Randolph-Sheppard Act of June 20, 1936, that the program has not developed, and has not been sustained, in the manner and spirit in which the Congress intended at the time of its enactment, and that, in fact, the growth of the program has been inhibited by a number of external forces;

(2) that the potential exists for doubling the number of blind operators on Federal and other property under the Randolph-Sheppard program within the next five years, provided the obstacles to growth are removed, that legislative and administrative means exist to remove such obstacles, and that Congress should adopt legislation to that end; and

(3) that at a minimum the following actions must be taken to insure the continued vitality and expansion of the Randolph-Sheppard program—

(A) establish uniformity of treatment of blind vendors by all Federal departments, agencies, and instrumentalities,

(B) establish guidelines for the operation of the program by State licensing agencies,

(C) require coordination among the several entities with responsibility for the program,

(D) establish a priority for vending facilities operated by blind vendors on Federal property,

(E) establish administrative and judicial procedures under which fair treatment of blind vendors, State licensing agencies, and the Federal Government is assured,

(F) require stronger administration and oversight functions in the Federal office carrying out the program, and

(G) accomplish other legislative and administrative objectives which will permit the Randolph-Sheppard program to flourish.

Randolph-Sheppard Act
as Amended December 7, 1974

AN ACT to authorize the operation of stands in Federal buildings by blind persons, to enlarge the economic opportunities of the blind, and for other purposes

Be it enacted by the Senate and House of Representatives of the United States of America in Congress assembled,

That (a) for the purposes of providing blind persons with remunerative employment, enlarging the economic opportunities of the blind, and stimulating the blind to greater efforts in striving to make themselves self-supporting, blind persons licensed under the provisions of this Act shall be authorized to operate vending facilities on any Federal property.

(b) In authorizing the operation of vending facilities on Federal property, priority shall be given to blind persons licensed by a State agency as provided in this Act; and the Secretary, through the Commissioner, shall, after consultation with the Administrator of General Services and other heads of departments, agencies, or instrumentalities of the United States in control of the maintenance, operation, and protection of Federal property, prescribe regulations designed to assure that—

(1) the priority under this subsection is given to such licensed blind persons (including assignment of vending machine income pursuant to section 7 of this Act to achieve and protect such priority), and

(2) wherever feasible, one or more vending facilities are established on all Federal property to the extent that any such facility or facilities would not adversely affect the interests of the United States.

Any limitation on the placement or operation of a vending facility based on a finding that such placement or operation would adversely affect the interests of the United States shall be fully justified in writing to the Secretary, who shall determine whether such limitation is justified. A determination made by the Secretary pursuant to this provision shall be binding on any department, agency, or instrumentality of the United States affected by such determination. The Secretary shall publish such determination, along with supporting documentation, in the Federal Register.

SEC. 2. (a) The Secretary of Health, Education, and Welfare shall—

(1) Insure that the Rehabilitation Services Administration is the principal agency for carrying out this Act; and the Commissioner shall, within one hundred and eighty days after enactment of the Randolph-Sheppard Amendments of 1974,[1] establish requirements for the uniform application of this Act by each State agency designated under paragraph (5) of this subsection, including appropriate accounting procedures, policies on the selection and establishment of new vending facilities, distribution of income to blind vendors, and the use and control of set-aside funds under section 3(3) of this Act;

(2) Through the Commissioner, make annual surveys of concession vending opportunities for blind persons on Federal and other property in the United States, particularly with respect to Federal property under the control of the General Services Administration, the Department of Defense, and the United States Postal Service;

(3) Make surveys throughout the United States of industries with a view to obtaining information that will assist blind persons to obtain employment;

(4) Make available to the public, and especially to persons and organizations engaged in work for the blind, information obtained as a result of such surveys;

(5) Designate as provided in section 3 of this Act the State agency for the blind in each State, or, in any State in which

1. Title II of Public Law 93-516, enacted December 7, 1974.

there is no such agency, some other public agency to issue licenses to blind persons who are citizens of the United States for the operating of vending facilities on Federal and other property in such State for the vending of newspapers, periodicals, confections, tobacco products, foods, beverages, and other articles or services dispensed automatically or manually and prepared on or off the premises in accordance with all applicable health laws, as determined by the State licensing agency, and including the vending or exchange of chances for any lottery authorized by State law and conducted by an agency of a State; and

(6) Through the Commissioner, (A) conduct periodic evaluations of the program authorized by this Act, including upward mobility and other training required by section 8, and annually submit to the appropriate committees of Congress a report based on such evaluations, and (B) take such other steps, including the issuance of such rules and regulations, as may be necessary or desirable in carrying out the provisions of this Act.

(b) The State licensing agency shall, in issuing each such license for the operation of a vending facility, give preference to blind persons who are in need of employment. Each such license shall be issued for an indefinite period but may be terminated by the State licensing agency if it is satisfied that the facility is not being operated in accordance with the rules and regulations prescribed by such licensing agency. Such licenses shall be issued only to applicants who are blind within the meaning of this Act.

(c) The State licensing agency designated by the Secretary is authorized, with the approval of the head of the department or agency in control of the maintenance, operation, and protection of the Federal property on which the facility is to be located but subject to regulations prescribed pursuant to the first section, to select a location for such facility and the type of facility to be provided.

(d) (1) After January 1, 1975, no department, agency, or

177

instrumentality of the United States shall undertake to acquire by ownership, rent, lease, or to otherwise occupy, in whole or in part, any building unless, after consultation with the head of such department, agency, or instrumentality and the State licensing agency, it is determined by the Secretary that (A) such building includes a satisfactory site or sites for the location and operation of a vending facility by a blind person, or (B) if a building is to be constructed, substantially altered, or renovated, or in the case of a building that is already occupied on such date by such department, agency, or instrumentality, is to be substantially altered or renovated for use by such department, agency, or instrumentality, the design for such construction, substantial alteration, or renovation includes a satisfactory site or sites for the location and operation of a vending facility by a blind person. Each such department, agency, or instrumentality shall provide notice to the appropriate State licensing agency of its plans for occupation, acquisition, renovation, or relocation of a building adequate to permit such State agency to determine whether such building includes a satisfactory site or sites for a vending facility.

(2) The provisions of paragraph (1) shall not apply (A) when the Secretary and the State licensing agency determine that the number of people using the property is or will be insufficient to support a vending facility, or (B) to any privately owned building, any part of which is leased by any department, agency, or instrumentality of the United States and in which, (i) prior to the execution of such lease, the lessor or any of his tenants had in operation a restaurant or other food facility in a part of the building not included in such lease, and (ii) the operation of such a vending facility by a blind person would be in proximate and substantial direct competition with such restaurant or other food facility except that each such department, agency, and instrumentality shall make every effort to lease property in privately owned buildings capable of accommodating a vending facility.

(3) For the purposes of this subsection, the term "satisfactory site" means an area determined by the Secretary to have sufficient space, electrical and plumbing outlets, and such other facilities as the Secretary may by regulation prescribe, for the location and operation of a vending facility by a blind person.

(e) In any State having an approved plan for vocational rehabilitation pursuant to the Vocational Rehabilitation Act or the Rehabilitation Act of 1973 (Public Law 93-112), the State licensing agency designated under paragraph (5) of subsection (a) of this section shall be the State agency designated under section 101 (a) (1) (A) of such Rehabilitation Act of 1973.

SEC. 3. A State agency for the blind or other State agency desiring to be designated as the licensing agency shall, with the approval of the chief executive of the State, make application to the Secretary and agree—

(1) to cooperate with the Secretary in carrying out the purpose of this Act;

(2) to provide for each licensed blind person such vending facility equipment, and adequate initial stock of suitable articles to be vended therefrom, as may be necessary: *Provided however,* That such equipment and stock may be owned by the licensing agency for use of the blind, or by the blind individual to whom the license is issued: *And provided further,* That if ownership of such equipment is vested in the blind licensee, (A) the State licensing agency shall retain a first option to repurchase such equipment and (B) in the event such individual dies or for any other reason ceases to be a licensee or transfers to another vending facility, ownership of such equipment shall become vested in the State licensing agency (for transfer to a successor licensee) subject to an obligation on the part of the State licensing agency to pay to such individual (or to his estate) the fair value of his interest therein as later determined in accordance with regulations of

179

the State licensing agency and after opportunity for a fair hearing;

(3) that if any funds are set aside, or caused to be set aside, from the net proceeds of the operation of the vending facilities such funds shall be set aside, or caused to be set aside, only to the extent necessary for and may be used only for the purposes of (A) maintenance and replacement of equipment; (B) the purchase of new equipment; (C) management services; (D) assuring a fair minimum return to operators of vending facilities; and (E) retirement or pension funds, health insurance contributions, and provision for paid sick leave and vacation time, if it is determined by a majority vote of blind licensees licensed by such State agency, after such agency provides to each such licensee full information on all matters relevant to such proposed program, that funds under this paragraph shall be set aside for such purposes: *Provided, however,* That in no event shall the amount of such funds to be set aside from the net proceeds of any vending facility exceed a reasonable amount which shall be determined by the Secretary;

(4) to make such reports in such form and containing such information as the Secretary may from time to time require and to comply with such provisions as he may from time to time find necessary to assure the correctness and verification of such reports;

(5) to issue such regulations, consistent with the provisions of this Act, as may be necessary for the operation of this program;

(6) to provide to any blind licensee dissatisfied with any action arising from the operation or administration of the vending facility program an opportunity for a fair hearing, and to agree to submit the grievances of any blind licensee not otherwise resolved by such hearing to arbitration as provided in section 5 of this Act.

SEC. 4. (a) The Secretary is authorized to make such expenditures out of any money appropriated therefor (including expenditures for personal services and rent at the seat of government and elsewhere, books of reference and periodicals, for printing and binding, and for traveling expenses) as he may deem necessary to carry out the provisions of this Act.

(b) The Secretary shall, in employing such additional personnel as may be necessary, give preference to blind persons who are capable of discharging the required duties.

SEC. 5. (a) Any blind licensee who is dissatisfied with any action arising from the operation or administration of the vending facility program may submit to a State licensing agency a request for a full evidentiary hearing, which shall be provided by such agency in accordance with section 3(6) of this Act. If such blind licensee is dissatisfied with any action taken or decision rendered as a result of such hearing, he may file a complaint with the Secretary who shall convene a panel to arbitrate the dispute pursuant to section 6 of this Act, and the decision of such panel shall be final and binding on the parties except as otherwise provided in this Act.

(b) Whenever any State licensing agency determines that any department, agency, or instrumentality of the United States that has control of the maintenance, operation, and protection of Federal property is failing to comply with the provisions of this Act or any regulations issued thereunder (including a limitation on the placement or operation of a vending facility as described in section 1(b) of this Act and the Secretary's determination thereon) such licensing agency may file a complaint with the Secretary who shall convene a panel to arbitrate the dispute pursuant to section 6 of this Act, and the decision of such panel shall be final and binding on the parties except as otherwise provided in this Act.

SEC. 6. (a) Upon receipt of a complaint filed under section 5 of this Act, the Secretary shall convene an ad hoc arbitration panel as provided in subsection (b). Such panel shall, in accordance with the provisions of subchapter II of chapter 5 of title 5, United States Code, give notice, conduct a hearing, and render its decision which shall be subject to appeal and

181

review as a final agency action for purposes of chapter 7 of such title 5.

(b)(1) The arbitration panel convened by the Secretary to hear grievances of blind licensees shall be composed of three members appointed as follows:

(A) one individual designated by the State licensing agency;

(B) one individual designated by the blind licensee; and

(C) one individual, not employed by the State licensing agency or, where appropriate, its parent agency, who shall serve as chairman, jointly designated by the members appointed under subparagraphs (A) and (B).

If any party fails to designate a member under subparagraph (1) (A), (B), or (C), the Secretary shall designate such member on behalf of such party.

(2) The arbitration panel convened by the Secretary to hear complaints filed by a State licensing agency shall be composed of three members appointed as follows:

(A) one individual, designated by the State licensing agency;

(B) one individual, designated by the head of the Federal department, agency, or instrumentality controlling the Federal property over which the dispute arose; and

(C) one individual, not employed by the Federal department, agency, or instrumentality controlling the Federal property over which the dispute arose, who shall serve as chairman, jointly designated by the members appointed under subparagraphs (A) and (B).

If any party fails to designate a member under subparagraph (2) (A), (B), or (C), the Secretary shall designate such member on behalf of such party. If the panel appointed pursuant to paragraph (2) finds that the acts or practices of any such department, agency, or instrumentality are in violation of this Act, or any regulation issued thereunder, the head of any such department, agency, or instrumentality shall cause such acts or practices to be terminated promptly and shall take such other action as may be necessary to carry out the decision of the panel.

(c) The decisions of a panel convened by the Secretary pursuant to this section shall be matters of public record and shall be published in the Federal Register.

(d) The Secretary shall pay all reasonable costs of arbitration under this section in accordance with a schedule of fees and expenses he shall publish in the Federal Register.

SEC. 7. (a) In accordance with the provisions of subsection (b) of this section, vending machine income obtained from the operation of vending machines on Federal property shall accrue (1) to the blind licensee operating a vending facility on such property, or (2) in the event there is no blind licensee operating such facility on such property, to the State agency in whose State the Federal property is located, for the uses designated in subsection (c) of this section, except that with respect to income which accrues under clause (1) of this subsection, the Commissioner may prescribe regulations imposing a ceiling on income from such vending machines for an individual blind licensee. In the event such a ceiling is imposed, no blind licensee shall receive less vending machine income under such ceiling than he was receiving on January 1, 1974. No limitation shall be imposed on income from vending machines, combined to create a vending facility, which are maintained, serviced, or operated by a blind licensee. Any amounts received by a blind licensee that are in excess of the amount permitted to accrue to him under any ceiling imposed by the Commissioner shall be disbursed to the appropriate State agency under clause (2) of this subsection and shall be used by such agency in accordance with subsection (c) of this section.

(b)(1) After January 1, 1975, 100 per centum of all vending machine income from vending machines on Federal property which are in direct competition with a blind vending facility shall accrue as specified in subsection (a) of this section. "Direct competition" as used in this section means the existence of any vending machines or facilities operated on the same premises as a blind vending facility except that vending machines or facilities operated in areas serving employees the majority of whom normally do not have direct access to the blind vending facility shall not be considered in direct competition with the blind vending facility. After January 1, 1975, 50 per centum of all vending machine income from vending machines on Federal property which are not in direct competition with a blind vending facility shall accrue as specified in subsection (a) of this section, except that with respect to Federal property at which at least 50 per centum of the total hours worked on the premises occurs during periods other than normal working hours, 30 per centum of such income shall so accrue.

(2) The head of each department, agency, and instrumentality of the United States shall insure compliance with this section with respect to buildings, installations, and facilities under his control, and shall be responsible for collection of, and accounting for, such vending machine income.

(c) All vending machine income which accrues to a State licensing agency pursuant to subsection (a) of this section shall be used to establish retirement or pension plans, for health insurance contributions, and for provision of paid sick leave and vacation time for blind licensees in such State, subject to a vote of blind licensees as provided under section 3(3) (E) of this Act. Any vending machine income remaining after application of the first sentence of this subsection shall be used for the purposes specified in sections 3(3) (A), (B), (C), and (D) of this Act, and any assessment charged to blind licensees by a State licensing agency shall be reduced pro rata in an amount equal to the total of such remaining vending machine income.

(d) Subsections (a) and (b) (1) of this section shall not apply to income from vending machines within retail sales outlets under the control of exchange or ships' stores systems authorized by title 10, United States Code, or to income

184

from vending machines operated by the Veterans Canteen Service, or to income from vending machines not in direct competition with a blind vending facility at individual locations, installations, or facilities on Federal property the total of which at such individual locations, installations, or facilities does not exceed $3,000 annually.

(e) The Secretary, through the Commissioner, shall prescribe regulations to establish a priority for the operation of cafeterias on Federal property by blind licensees when he determines, on an individual basis and after consultation with the head of the appropriate installation, that such operation can be provided at a reasonable cost with food of a high quality comparable to that currently provided to employees, whether by contract or otherwise.

(f) This section shall not operate to preclude preexisting or future arrangements, or regulations of departments, agencies, or instrumentalities of the United States, under which blind licensees (1) receive a greater percentage or amount of vending machine income than that specified in subsection (b) (1) of this section, or (2) receive vending machine income from individual locations, installations, or facilities on Federal property the total of which at such individual locations, installations, or facilities does not exceed $3,000 annually.

(g) The Secretary shall take such action and promulgate such regulations as he deems necessary to assure compliance with this section.

SEC. 8. The Commissioner shall insure, through promulgation of appropriate regulations, that uniform and effective training programs, including on-the-job training, are provided for blind individuals, through services under the Rehabilitation Act of 1973 (Public Law 93-112). He shall further insure that State agencies provide programs for upward mobility (including further education and additional training or retraining for improved work opportunities) for all trainees under this Act, and that follow-along services are provided to such trainees to assure that their maximum vocational potential is achieved.

SEC. 9. As used in this Act—

(1) "blind person" means a person whose central visual acuity does not exceed 20/200 in the better eye with correcting lenses or whose visual acuity, if better than 20/200, is accompanied by a limit to the field of vision in the better eye to such a degree that its widest diameter subtends an angle of no greater than twenty degrees. In determining whether an individual is blind, there shall be an examination by a physician skilled in diseases of the eye, or by an optometrist, whichever the individual shall select;

(2) "Commissioner" means the Commissioner of the Rehabilitation Services Administration;

(3) "Federal property" means any building, land, or other real property owned, leased, or occupied by any department, agency, or instrumentality of the United States (including the Department of Defense and the United States Postal Service), or any other instrumentality wholly owned by the United States, or by any department or agency of the District of Columbia or any territory or possession of the United States;

(4) "Secretary" means the Secretary of Health, Education, and Welfare;

(5) "State" means a State, territory, possession, Puerto Rico, or the District of Columbia;

(6) "United States" includes the several States, territories, and possessions of the United States, Puerto Rico, and the District of Columbia;

(7) "vending facility" means automatic vending machines, cafeterias, snack bars, cart services, shelters, counters, and such other appropriate auxiliary equipment as the Secretary may by regulation prescribe as being necessary for the sale of the articles or services described in section 2(a)(5) of this Act and which may be operated by blind licensees; and

186

(8) "vending machine income" means receipts (other than those of a blind licensee) from vending machine operations on Federal property, after cost of goods sold (including reasonable service and maintenance costs), where the machines are operated, serviced, or maintained by, or with the approval of, a department, agency, or instrumentality of the United States, or commissions paid (other than to a blind licensee) by a commercial vending concern which operates, services, and maintains vending machines on Federal property for, or with the approval of, a department, agency, or instrumentality of the United States.

SEC. 10. (a) The Secretary of Health, Education, and Welfare is directed to assign to the Office for the Blind and Visually Handicapped of the Rehabilitation Services Administration of the Department of Health, Education, and Welfare ten additional full-time personnel (or their equivalent), five of whom shall be supportive personnel, to carry out duties related to the administration of the Randolph-Sheppard Act.

(b) In selecting personnel to fill any position under this section, the Secretary of Health, Education, and Welfare shall give preference to blind individuals.

SEC. 11. In addition to other requirements imposed in this title[1] and in the Randolph-Sheppard Act upon State licensing agencies, such agencies shall—

(1) provide to each blind licensee access to all relevant financial data, including quarterly and annual financial reports, on the operation of the State vending facility program;

(2) conduct the biennial election of a Committee of Blind Vendors who shall be fully representative of all blind licensees in the State program, and

(3) insure that such committee's responsibilities include (A) participation, with the State agency, in major administrative decisions and policy and program development, (B)

1. Title II of Public Law 93-516, enacted December 7, 1974.

receiving grievances of blind licensees and serving as advocates for such licensees, (C) participation, with the State agency, in the development and administration of a transfer and promotion system for blind licensees, (D) participation, with the State agency, in developing training and retraining programs, and (E) sponsorship, with the assistance of the State agency, of meetings and instructional conferences for blind licensees.

SEC. 12. (a) The Secretary, through the Commissioner, after a period of study not to exceed six months following the date of enactment of this title,[1] and after full consultation with, and full consideration of the views of, blind vendors and State licensing agencies, shall promulgate national standards for funds set aside pursuant to section 3(3) of the Randolph-Sheppard Act which include maximum and minimum amounts for such funds, and appropriate contributions, if any, to such funds by blind vendors.

(b)(1) The Secretary shall study the feasibility and desirability of establishing a nationally administered retirement, pension, and health insurance system for blind licensees, and such study shall include, but not be limited to, consideration of eligibility standards, amounts and sources of contributions, number of potential participants, total costs, and alternative forms of administration, including trust funds and revolving funds.

(2) The Secretary shall, within one year following the date of enactment of this title,[1] complete the study required by paragraph (1) of this subsection and report his findings, together with any recommendations, to the President and the Congress.

(c) The Secretary shall, not later than September 30, 1975, complete an evaluation of the method of assigning vending machine income under section 7(b)(1) of the Randolph-Sheppard Act, including its effect on the growth of the pro-

1. Title II of Public Law 93-516, enacted December 7, 1974.

gram authorized by the Act, and on the operation of non-appropriated fund activities, and within thirty days thereafter he shall report his findings, together with any recommendations, to the appropriate committees of the Congress.

(d) Each State licensing agency shall, within one year following the date of enactment of this title,[1] submit to the Secretary a report, with appropriate supporting documentation, which shows the actions taken by such agency to meet the requirements of section 2(a)(1) of the Randolph-Sheppard Act.

SEC. 13. The Comptroller General is authorized to conduct regular and periodic audits of all nonappropriated fund activities which receive income from vending machines on Federal property, under such rules and regulations as he may prescribe. In the conduct of such audits he and his duly authorized representatives shall have access to any relevant books, documents, papers, accounts, and records of such activities as he deems necessary.

EDITOR'S NOTE: *Assignment of section numbers to the foregoing sections 10 through 13 was made by the editor. The numbering of these sections in the official edition of the Act may differ.*

The requirement in Section 4 (b) of the Randolph-Sheppard Act of 1936 that "at least 50 per centum of such additional personnel shall be blind persons" is deleted by Section 208 (d) of Public Law 93-516.

Included as Section 208 (b) of Public Law 93-516 is the following amendment to Section 5108 (c) of title 5, United States Code, dealing with Personnel:

(1) striking out "and" at the end of paragraph (10);

(2) striking out the period at the end of paragraph (11) and inserting in lieu thereof "; and"; and

1. Title II of Public Law 93-516, enacted December 7, 1974.

(3) adding after paragraph (11) the following new paragraph:

"(12) the Secretary of Health, Education, and Welfare, subject to the standards and procedures prescribed by this chapter, may place one additional position in the Office for the Blind and Visually Handicapped of the Rehabilitation Services Administration in GS-16, GS-17, or GS-18."